GCSE OCR Gateway
Extension Science
Higher Workbook

This book is for anyone doing **GCSE OCR Gateway Extension Science** at higher level.

It's full of **tricky questions**... each one designed to make you **sweat** — because that's the only way you'll get any **better**.

There are questions to see **what facts** you know. There are questions to see how well you can **apply those facts**. And there are questions to see what you know about **how science works**.

It's also got some daft bits in to try and make the whole experience at least vaguely entertaining for you.

What CGP is all about

Our sole aim here at CGP is to produce the highest quality books — carefully written, immaculately presented and dangerously close to being funny.

Then we work our socks off to get them out to you — at the cheapest possible prices.

Contents

Module B5 — The Living Body

Module B6 — Beyond the Microscope

Module C5 — How Much?

Module C6 — Chemistry Out There

Module P5 — Space for Reflection

Module P6 — Electricity for Gadgets

Published by CGP

Editors:
Luke Antieul, Katie Braid, Joe Brazier, Emma Elder, Mary Falkner, Murray Hamilton, David Hickinson, Edmund Robinson, Helen Ronan, Lyn Setchell, Jane Towle, Julie Wakeling.

Contributors:
Mike Bossart, Steve Coggins, Mike Dagless, Mark A Edwards, Derek Harvey, Frederick Langridge, Philip Rushworth, Pat Szczesniak, Paul Warren.

ISBN: 978 1 84762 860 2

With thanks to Charlotte Burrows, Ben Fletcher, Ian Francis, Julie Jackson, Jamie Sinclair, Hayley Thompson and Sarah Williams for the proofreading.

With thanks to Jan Greenway, Laura Jakubowski and Laura Stoney for the copyright research.

Groovy website: www.cgpbooks.co.uk

Printed by Elanders Ltd, Newcastle upon Tyne.
Jolly bits of clipart from CorelDRAW®
Based on the classic CGP style created by Richard Parsons.

Bones and Cartilage

Q1 Vertebrates have an **internal skeleton** whereas insects have an external one. Give three advantages of an internal skeleton.

1. ....

2. ....

3. ....

Q2 The diagram below shows a **long bone**.

a) Name the parts **A**, **B** and **C** on the diagram.

A .... B .... C ....

b) What is part **A** covered with?

....

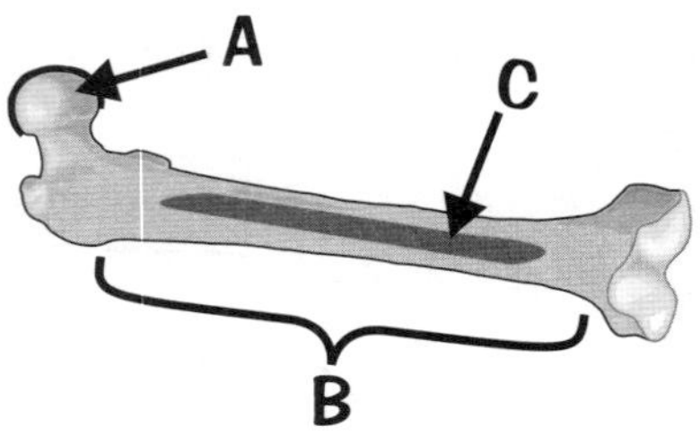

c) Long bones are **hollow**. Give one **advantage** of this.

....

....

Q3 Complete the passage about **bones** and **cartilage** using the words below.

infected	cartilage	knock	grow	calcium	phosphorus	broken	bone	repair	ossification

Bones and cartilage are made up of living cells — this allows them to .... and .... themselves, but it also means that they can become ....

Bones are strong, but they can be .... by a sharp ....

In the womb, bones start off as cartilage. They turn to bone when .... and .... are deposited as you grow. This process is called ....

In people who are still growing, there is a lot of .... present.

Q4 Elderly people often suffer from a disease called **osteoporosis**. Their bones are more prone to **fractures**.

a) Why are their bones more likely to break?

....

....

b) Explain why you should try to avoid moving anyone who might have a fracture.

....

Joints and Muscles

Q1 Complete the passage below to explain how different **joints** allow different ranges of movement.

socket   hinge   ball   rotate   one

.... joints, such as the knee and elbow, allow movement in .... direction only. .... and .... joints, for example the hip and shoulder, allow movement in many directions — they can also ....

Q2 Draw lines to match each part of a **synovial joint** to its function.

Cartilage	Hold the bones together
Synovial membrane	Acts as a shock absorber
Ligaments	Lubricates the joint
Synovial fluid	Produces synovial fluid

Q3 The diagram on the right is of a human **arm**.

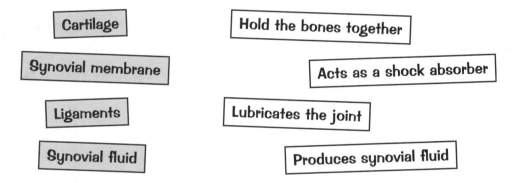

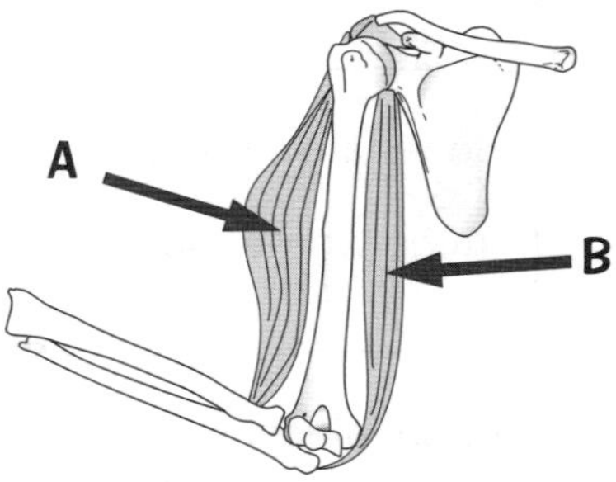

a) Name the muscles **A** and **B** on the diagram.

A .... B ....

b) Name the part of the arm that acts as a **pivot**.

....

c) Give the letter of the muscle that is **contracted** in the diagram. ....

d) Give the letter of the muscle that is **relaxed** in the diagram. ....

e) Describe how the antagonistic muscles A and B cause the arm to **straighten**.

....

Top Tips: There are loads of different types of joints but you only need to know about two — hinge, and ball and socket... so get them learnt. Don't forget that muscles usually work in pairs.

Circulatory Systems

Q1 Complete the passage using the words provided below.

diffusion	small	oxygen	large	circulatory
glucose	slow	waste	fast	

The cells of all living organisms need to be supplied with .... and .... They also need to get rid of .... like carbon dioxide. Single-celled organisms are small enough that these materials can move in and out by ...., but multicellular organisms are so .... that diffusion would be too .... Because of this, they need a .... system to move materials more efficiently around the body.

Q2 Complete the sentences below by circling the correct word(s) from the choices given.

a) Arteries carry blood **away from** / **towards** the heart under **low** / **high** pressure.

b) Veins carry blood **away from** / **towards** the heart under **low** / **high** pressure.

Q3 The diagram below shows how **blood pressure** changes as blood flows around the body.

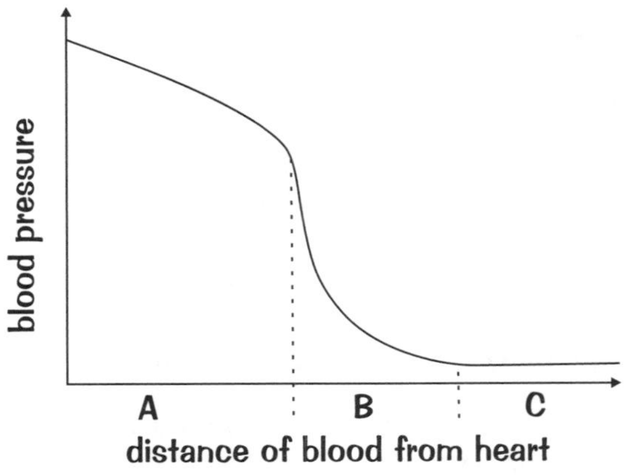

Blood was under a lot of pressure revising for his exams.

a) What happens to blood pressure as blood flows away from the heart?

....

b) Name the types of blood vessels **A**, **B** and **C** on the diagram.

A .... B .... C ....

Circulatory Systems

Q4 Organisms can have a **single** or **double** circulatory system.

a) Draw lines to match each organism to the correct type of circulatory system and its description.

fish	single circulatory system	two circuits of blood vessels from the heart
mammals	double circulatory system	one circuit of blood vessels from the heart

b) **i)** Explain why organisms with a **single circulatory system** have a **two-chambered heart**.

....

....

ii) Explain why organisms with a **double circulatory system** have a **four-chambered heart**.

....

....

Q5 Tick the boxes next to the following statements to show whether they're **true** or **false**.

		True	False
a)	Unborn babies don't need a double circulatory system.	☐	☐
b)	Unborn babies get their oxygen from their mother via the placenta.	☐	☐
c)	In unborn babies, blood travels from the heart to the lungs and then on to the rest of the body.	☐	☐
d)	All unborn babies have a hole in the heart, which closes just before birth.	☐	☐

Q6 In a double circulatory system blood is under **high pressure**.

a) Explain why blood pressure is higher in the body of organisms with a double circulatory system than those with a single circulatory system.

....

....

....

b) Give one **advantage** of having higher blood pressure.

....

The Cardiac Cycle and Circulation

Q1 The **cardiac cycle** is the sequence of events that takes place in one complete heartbeat.

The sentences below describe some of these events. Number them to show their correct order.

☐ Blood flows into the pulmonary artery and aorta.

1 Blood flows into the atria from the vena cava and pulmonary vein.

☐ The ventricles contract.

☐ The cycle starts again as blood flows into the atria.

☐ The atria contract, pushing blood into the ventricles.

The first one has been done for you.

Q2 For each of the following stages of the cardiac cycle, tick the boxes to show whether the semilunar and atrio-ventricular valves are **open** or **closed**.

a) Blood flows into the atria.

	Open	Closed
Semilunar valves	☐	☐
Atrio-ventricular valves	☐	☐

b) The ventricles contract.

	Open	Closed
Semilunar valves	☐	☐
Atrio-ventricular valves	☐	☐

c) The atria contract.

	Open	Closed
Semilunar valves	☐	☐
Atrio-ventricular valves	☐	☐

Q3 We understand how the circulatory system works thanks to the work of **William Harvey**.

a) Give **two** things that William Harvey discovered.

....

....

b) How did Claudius Galen's idea of how the circulatory system works differ from Harvey's idea?

....

....

....

....

Eureka! I've discovered the chambers of the heart!
It's all Greek to me...

Heart Rate

Q1 Your **heart rate** changes depending on your level of activity. The graph below shows the heart rate of a student who sprints for a bus.

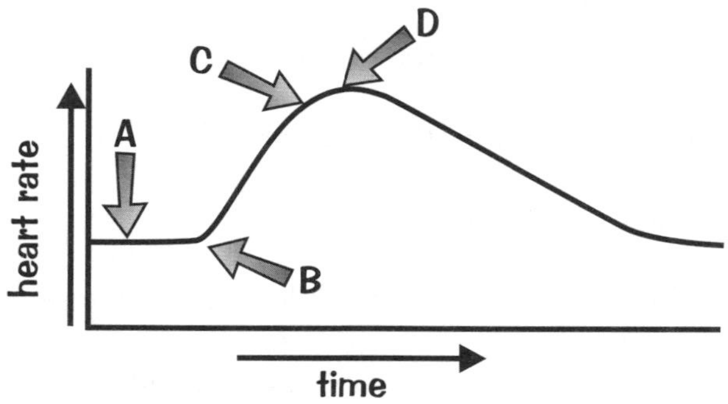

After a brisk walk in the countryside, Kate's art rate increased dramatically.

a) i) At what point, **A**, **B**, **C** or **D**, does he start to run?

....

ii) At what point, **A**, **B**, **C** or **D**, does he stop running?

....

b) Suggest an **advantage** of an increased heart rate during sprinting.

....

c) Which **hormone** can also cause your heart rate to increase?

....

Q2 Complete the passage about the **heart's pacemaker**, using the words below.

Some words may be used more than once.

skin	SAN	muscle	electric current	atria	AVN	wire	contract	ventricles

A small .... is generated by the .... The current spreads through the .... cells of the .... making them .... The current then stimulates the .... to produce an .... This current spreads through the .... cells of the .... making them .... In this way, the .... always contract before the .... If the pacemaker cells don't work properly the .... can be generated by an artificial pacemaker implanted under the .... and connected to the heart by a ....

Heart Rate

Q3 The diagrams below show **ECG recordings** from a healthy person and a person admitted to hospital with a heart problem.

a) What is recorded by the ECG trace?

....

b) Which parts of the cardiac cycle do the labels **A**, **B**, **C** and **D** represent?

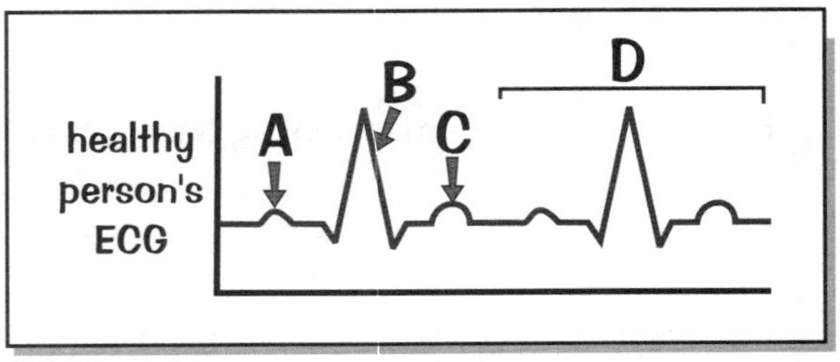

A ....

B ....

C ....

D ....

c) How does the ECG trace of the hospital patient **differ** from that of the healthy person?

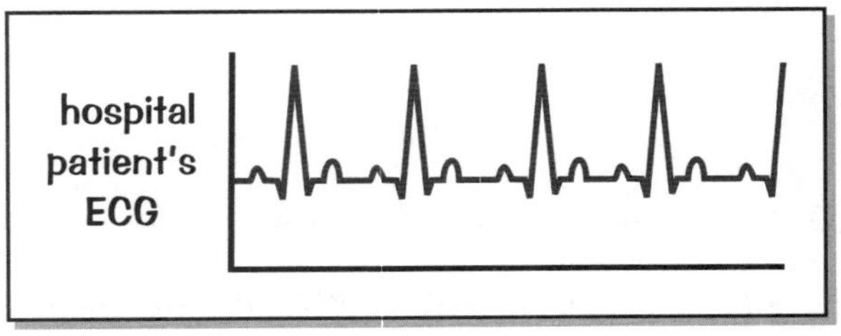

....

....

d) Give one heart problem an ECG is commonly used to detect.

....

Q4 **Echocardiograms** can also be used to investigate heart function.

a) What is an echocardiogram? Tick the correct box.

☐ An X-ray of the heart.

☐ A way of measuring the blood pressure of the heart chambers.

☐ An ultrasound scan of the heart.

b) Suggest one heart problem that echocardiograms can be used to detect.

....

Top Tips: There could well be a question on ECGs in the exam so it's crucial that you know what they are used for, how to label one and how to identify different problems from them.

Heart Disease

Q1 **Surgery** is often used to correct heart problems.

a) Draw lines to match each heart condition to the problems it causes and the correct treatment.

Valve damage	reduces blood flow to the heart muscle	coronary bypass surgery
Coronary Heart Disease	blood doesn't circulate as effectively as normal	replacement by artificial valves

b) Describe what happens in a **coronary bypass** operation.

....

....

c) When might a **heart assist device** be used?

....

Q2 Some people suffer from a **hole in the heart.**

a) **i)** Describe the condition known as a 'hole in the heart'.

....

ii) What effect can it have on the circulation of blood in the heart?

....

b) Explain how a hole in the heart results in less oxygen in the blood.

....

c) How can a hole in the heart be corrected?

....

Q3 **Heart pacemakers** and **valves** can be used to treat heart disease instead of a heart transplant.

a) Give **one advantage** of fitting heart pacemakers and valves compared with heart transplants.

....

b) Give **one disadvantage** of fitting heart pacemakers and valves compared with heart transplants.

....

Blood Clotting and Transfusions

Q1 When you are cut, your blood **clots** so that you don't lose too much.

a) What is a **blood clot**?

....

b) How is a blood clot **formed**?

....

....

Q2 Use the words below to complete the passage about **blood clotting disorders**.

heparin	haemophilia	inherited	warfarin	prevent	aspirin

Strokes and DVT are conditions caused by excessive blood clotting. People at risk of these conditions take drugs such as .... , ... and .... to help .... blood clotting. .... is an .... disease in which the blood takes longer to clot. It can be treated with injections of a clotting factor.

Q3 There are four different **blood groups**, which are determined by the **antigens** present on a person's red blood cells.

a) Name the **four** blood groups. ....

b) What is an **antigen**?

....

c) What is **agglutination**?

....

d) Where in the blood are **antibodies** found?
Tick the correct answer.

- [ ] On red blood cells
- [ ] On the platelets
- [ ] In the plasma

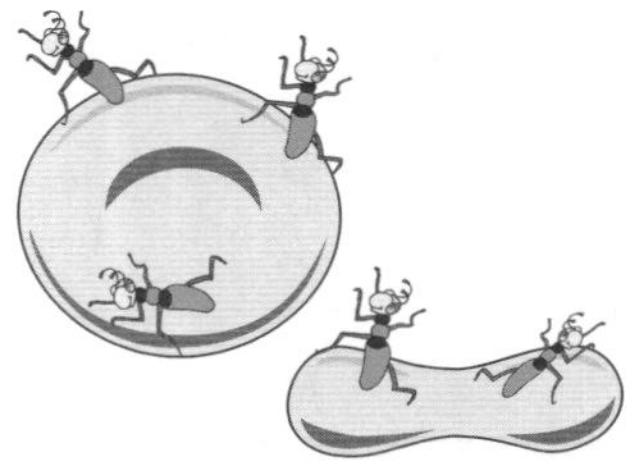

Blood Clotting and Transfusions

Q4 Complete the table below to show which blood groups have which **antigens** and which **antibodies**.

Blood group	Antigens present	Antibodies present
		anti-B
	B	
AB		
	none	

Q5 The presence or absence of blood group antigens determines who can receive **blood transfusions** from certain donors.

a) In what situation might you need a blood transfusion?

....

Use the table you have just filled in to help you.

b) Circle the correct answer to show whether a person can **receive** or **donate** a particular blood group.

i)	If they are blood group **A** can they **receive** blood group **B**?	**yes / no**
ii)	If they are blood group **A** can they **receive** blood group **O**?	**yes / no**
iii)	If they are blood group **AB** can they **receive** blood group **B**?	**yes / no**
iv)	If they are blood group **AB** can they **donate** to blood group **B**?	**yes / no**

c) Which blood group can donate their blood to any other blood group? ....

d) Which blood group can only receive blood of the same blood type? ....

e) Explain why a person with blood group A can't accept blood from a person with blood group B.

....

....

Q6 When blood is donated it is collected in a bag containing a substance called **heparin**.

Suggest a reason why heparin is present.

....

Top Tips: You might be asked to interpret data on blood transfusions in the exam — don't panic, think about the antigens and antibodies present and draw a table if it helps you figure it out.

Transplants and Organ Donation

Q1 Both living and dead people can donate organs but have to meet certain **criteria** to do so.

a) **i)** Name an organ that could be donated by a living donor. ....

ii) Give **two** criteria that living donors must meet to donate an organ.

....

b) Describe the criteria that a dead person must meet to donate an organ.

....

....

Q2 Complete the passage by choosing from the words below.

skill   drugs   age   success   rejection   organ   surgery

Transplants are risky in general because they involve major .... but .... rates depend on a lot of factors. The type of .... transplanted is important, as are the .... of the patient and the .... of the surgeon. Even if all goes well there can be problems caused by .... or by taking immuno-suppressive ....

Q3 The table below shows the number of **heart transplants** carried out in Cloudyford.

Year	1996	1997	1998	1999	2000	2001	2002	2003	2004	2005
No. heart transplants	36	35	35	31	30	27	24	21	26	20

a) Plot these figures as a bar chart on the grid on the right.

b) Describe how the number of heart transplants has changed over time.

....

....

c) Suggest why the future number of transplants carried out in Cloudyford may:

i) increase. ....

ii) decrease. ....

Organ Donation and Organ Replacement

Q1 There **aren't enough donors** to provide organs for all the people who need them.

a) Tick the boxes next to the factors below that explain why there are problems in the supply of organs.

- ☐ There's a shortage of people willing to be donors.
- ☐ Some donated organs will be the wrong colour.
- ☐ Not all donated organs will be the right tissue match for the patient who needs them.
- ☐ Patients are picky about which organs they'll accept.
- ☐ Donors must be roughly the same size and age as the patient who needs their organs.

b) Some countries have a **register** of people willing to donate organs after their death.

i) Suggest one **advantage** of having a register of donors.

....

ii) Suggest one **problem** with a register of donors.

....

Q2 Temporary **mechanical replacement organs** can be used to keep people alive.

a) Give **one** example of a temporary mechanical replacement for an organ.

....

b) Give four **problems** with using mechanical replacements for organs.

1. ....
2. ....
3. ....
4. ....

Top Tips: The average waiting time for an adult kidney transplant in the UK is around three years. Waiting times for different organs vary, but all are affected by the shortage of organ donors.

The Respiratory System

Q1 Complete the following sentences by circling the correct word in each pair.

a) Carbon dioxide is **beneficial** / **toxic** to the body at a **low** / **high** level.

b) When the **brain** / **nose** detects a rise in the carbon dioxide level it responds by **decreasing** / **increasing** the rate of breathing.

Q2 The following statements describe events which take place during either **inspiration** (breathing in) or **expiration** (breathing out):

- Intercostal muscles and diaphragm contract
- Thorax volume increases
- Air is pushed out of the lungs
- Pressure in lungs increases
- Pressure in lungs decreases
- Thorax volume decreases
- Diaphragm and intercostal muscles relax
- Air enters the lungs

Place the statements into the correct columns in the right order.

Inspiration	Expiration

Q3 Doctors measure **lung capacity** to help diagnose and monitor lung diseases.

a) What **machine** do they use to measure lung capacity? ....

b) What is the total volume of air you breathe in during a normal breath called? ....

c) What is **vital capacity air**? ....

d) At point **A** on the graph draw:

i) One normal breath in.

ii) Then one big breath out.

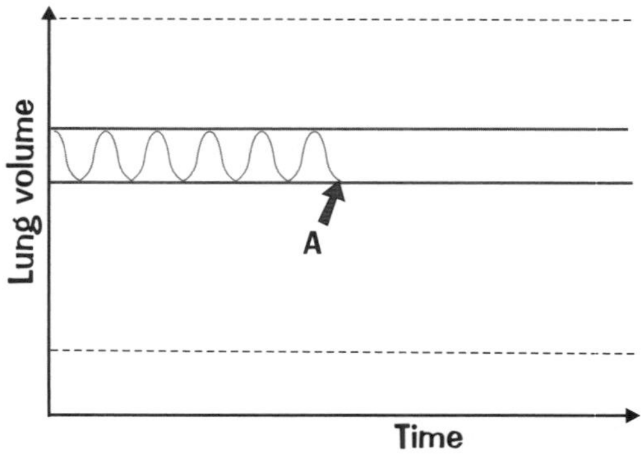

More on the Respiratory System

Q1 Gas exchange in humans occurs in the **alveoli**.

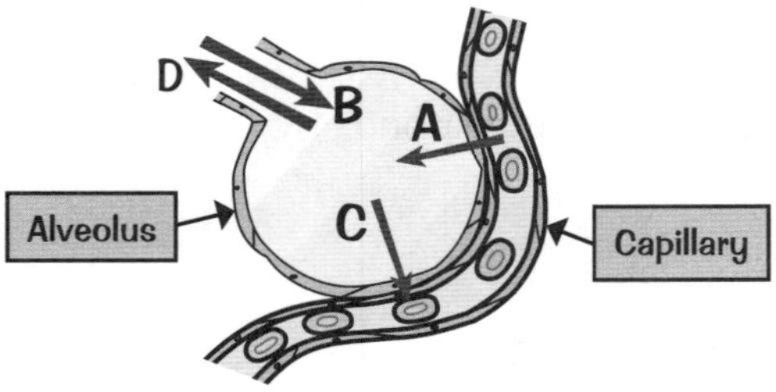

a) Match the labels A-D with the following statements:

i) air in ☐

ii) air out ☐

iii) movement of CO_2 ☐

iv) movement of O_2 ☐

b) By what **process** does the exchange of oxygen and carbon dioxide occur?

....

Q2 The alveoli are adapted to ensure **efficient** gas exchange.

Describe **four** features of the alveoli which make gas exchange as efficient as possible.

1. ....

2. ....

3. ....

4. ....

Q3 **Amphibians** and **fish** have different methods of gas exchange from humans.

a) **i)** How do adult **amphibians** exchange oxygen and carbon dioxide?

....

ii) How and why does this restrict where they can live?

....

....

b) **i)** Complete the paragraph by circling the correct words.

In **fish** / **reptiles** gas exchange occurs at the **mouth** / **gills**. Water rich in oxygen flows in through the mouth and is forced over the gill **filaments** / **fibres** when the mouth closes.

ii) Why are **fish** unable to breathe out of water?

....

....

Lung Disease

Q1 The respiratory tract is lined with a **mucous membrane**.

a) What is the function of the following?

i) Mucus ....

ii) Cilia ....

b) Name two parts of the respiratory tract where the mucus and cilia are found.

1. .... 2. ....

c) The respiratory tract leads to the lungs. Why are the lungs particularly prone to infection?

....

Q2 Lung diseases have many causes. For the following diseases give a **cause** (e.g. lifestyle, industrial or genetic) and describe the illness.

a) Cystic fibrosis ....

....

b) Asbestosis ....

....

c) Lung cancer ....

....

Q3 Complete the following passage about **asthma** by filling in the blanks using the words below.

wheezing	lining	difficult	inhaler	inflamed	contract	a tight chest	muscles

Asthma sufferers' lungs are overly sensitive to things such as pollen or dust. These cause the .... of the airways to become .... and fluid to build up in the airways. The .... around the bronchioles ...., narrowing the airways and making it .... to breathe. Symptoms include shortness of breath, ... and .... To control attacks asthmatics take drugs , usually administered by an ....

Digestion

Q1 Tick the box next to the statement which is **true**.

Small soluble molecules in food need to be assembled into large molecules before they can pass into your blood plasma or lymph. ☐

Large insoluble molecules in food need to be broken down into small molecules, so they can pass more easily into your blood plasma or lymph. ☐

Large insoluble molecules in food need to be broken down into small molecules, so they can pass more easily into your intestines. ☐

Q2 Complete the table to show where the following **digestive enzymes** are active in the body.

	Active in...	Also active in...
Carbohydrases		
Proteases		
Lipases		

Q3 Fill in the boxes to show how the **three main food groups** are **broken down** during digestion.

a)

[ ]
↓
protein → [ ]

Start digesting sooner with Lipase Lipstick.

b)

lipase
↓
[ ] → [ ] + [ ]

c)

[ ]
↓ ↓
[ ] → maltose → [ ]

Q4 Explain the importance of **physical digestion**.

....

....

More on Digestion

Q1 Use the words provided to complete the passage below.

alkaline   protease   small intestine   acidic

The pH in the stomach is very .... It's maintained at this level to provide the optimum pH for .... enzymes.
Other enzymes have different optimum pHs and so need different conditions — for example, the mouth and .... are .... so the enzymes found there can function properly.

Q2 Circle the correct word(s) in each pair to complete this passage about **bile**.

Bile is stored in the **gall bladder** / **pancreas** before being released into the small intestine.
Bile **acidifies** / **neutralises** the material from the stomach so that it is the optimum pH for the **enzymes** / **microorganisms** in the rest of the digestive system to work.
Bile also helps digest **fat** / **glycerol** by breaking it down into tiny droplets.
This is called **emulsification** / **reduction** and it gives a much bigger surface area for **carbohydrase** / **lipase** enzymes to work on.

Q3 Describe how the products of **digestion** move into the blood and lymph.

....

....

....

Q4 Describe two features of the **small intestine** that make it well-adapted to the absorption of food.

1. ....

....

2. ....

....

Top Tips Digestion is about getting all the **nutrients** from your food into your blood. The nutrients need to be broken down into **small molecules** first, so that they can be easily absorbed.

The Kidneys

Q1 The diagram below shows the human **kidneys**. The renal vein has been labelled. Complete the remaining labels **a)** to **d)**.

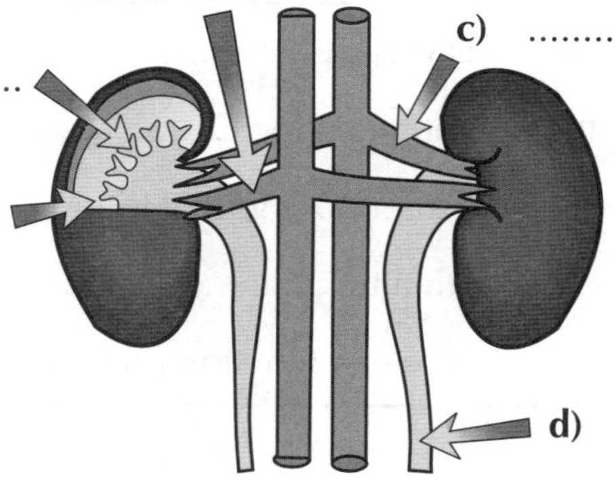

b) ....

c) ....

a) ....

d) ....

Q2 The kidney is involved in the **excretion** of wastes from the body. One of these wastes is **urea**.

a) **i)** Where is urea produced?

....

ii) What is urea produced from?

....

b) Briefly explain how the kidneys excrete wastes from the body.

....

c) What is the end product of excretion?

....

Q3 Complete the passage using some of the words provided below.

glomerulus **selectively** **proteins** **salt**
randomly **urea** **nephron** **ADH** **capsule**

Some words may be used more than once.

Water, ... and salt are squeezed out of the blood and into the .... under high pressure. Membranes between the blood vessels in the .... and the .... act like filters, so big molecules like proteins are not squeezed out. As the liquid flows along the .... useful substances are .... reabsorbed. How much water is reabsorbed is regulated by the hormone .... is also .... reabsorbed.

Waste Removal

Q1 The concentration of water in the blood is adjusted by the **kidneys**. They ensure that the water content never gets **too high** or **too low**.

a) What is the name given to the **mechanism** by which water content is regulated?

....

b) Complete the diagram below by circling the correct word in each pair.

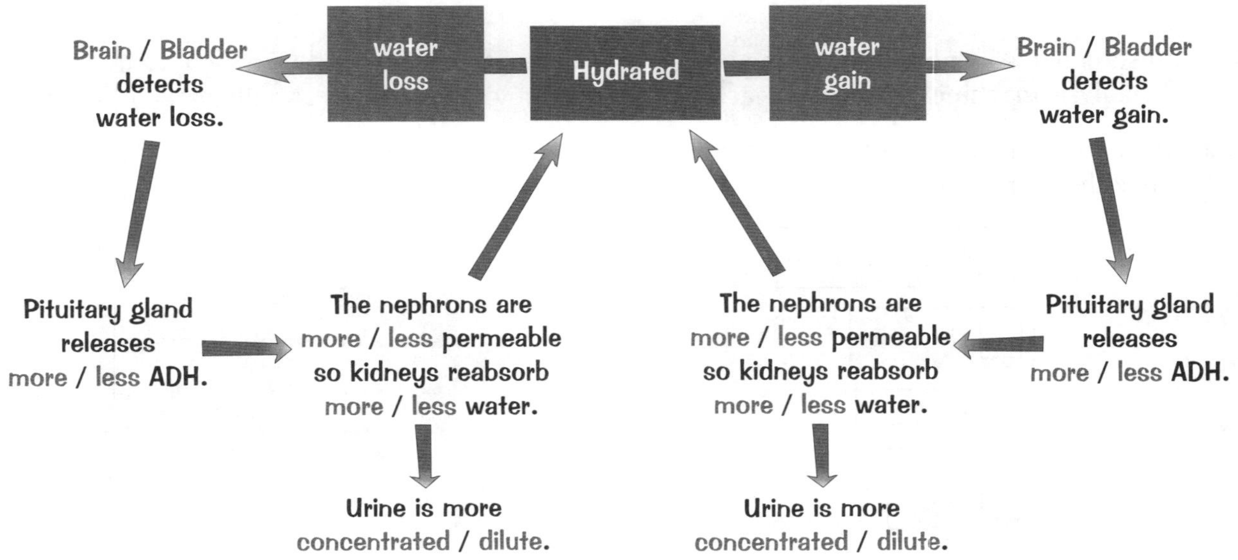

Brain / Bladder detects water loss.
water loss
Hydrated
water gain
Brain / Bladder detects water gain.
Pituitary gland releases more / less ADH.
The nephrons are more / less permeable so kidneys reabsorb more / less water.
The nephrons are more / less permeable so kidneys reabsorb more / less water.
Pituitary gland releases more / less ADH.
Urine is more concentrated / dilute.
Urine is more concentrated / dilute.

Q2 The concentration of urine and amount of urine produced are affected by many factors.

a) List three things that determine the **amount** and **concentration** of urine.

1. ....

2. ....

3. ....

b) Complete the following sentences by circling the correct words.

i) When you drink too little you will produce **more concentrated** / **less concentrated** urine.

ii) On a hot day you will produce **more concentrated** / **less concentrated** urine than on a cold day.

iii) Drinking a lot of water will produce a **large** / **small** amount of urine.

iv) Drinking a lot of water will produce **dilute** / **concentrated** urine.

v) Exercising will produce **more concentrated** / **less concentrated** urine than resting will.

c) Why does **exercising** change the concentration of urine produced?

....

....

Waste Removal

Q3 Explain why it's important to keep the concentration of water molecules in the blood plasma **constant**.

....

....

Q4 If someone's kidneys fail they may be given a **kidney transplant** or they may have to use a **dialysis machine**. A dialysis machine does the job of the kidneys and filters the blood.

a) What substances would you expect a dialysis machine to remove from the blood? Tick the correct boxes.

- ☐ Excess sodium
- ☐ Glucose
- ☐ Proteins
- ☐ Urea

The new kidney opera house was less popular than the old one.

b) Add the correct labels to the dialysis diagram.

A Blood returned to patient
B Dialysis fluid in
C Selectively permeable barrier
D Dialysis fluid out
E Blood from patient

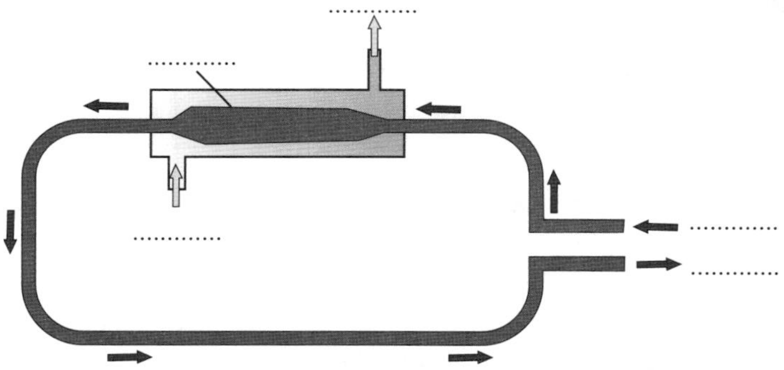

c) **i)** **How** does the composition of dialysis fluid compare with the composition of blood plasma?

....

ii) Why is this important?

....

Top Tips: Dialysis is a clever technique that's saved lives. The problem is that it can take up to four hours to filter the blood and it has to be done a couple of times a week. An alternative is a kidney transplant — you can live with only one kidney, so it's possible for some people with kidney failure to receive a donated organ from a member of their family.

The Menstrual Cycle

Q1 The menstrual cycle is controlled by four hormones: **FSH**, **LH**, **progesterone** and **oestrogen**.

a) Complete the table below to show the effects of these by placing ticks in the correct boxes.

Effect	FSH	LH	Progesterone	Oestrogen
Causes the lining of the uterus to repair (thicken and grow)				
Causes egg to develop in ovaries				
Controls ovulation				
Maintains uterus lining				

b) Which of the hormones above are released by the pituitary gland?

....

c) What do the following letters stand for?

i) FSH: ....

ii) LH: ....

Q2 When the concentration of one hormone becomes too high, the release of another hormone returns it to a lower level.

a) What is the name given to the **mechanism** by which hormones involved in the menstrual cycle are controlled?

....

b) Draw lines to complete the following sentences.

Progesterone inhibits the release of	progesterone.
Oestrogen inhibits the release of	oestrogen.
LH indirectly stimulates the production of	LH.
FSH stimulates the ovaries to produce	FSH.

Controlling Fertility

Q1 A variety of infertility treatments are available to help people who can't conceive naturally.

a) Tick the correct boxes to show whether the following statements about infertility treatments are **true** or **false**.

	True	False
i) Artificial insemination can use sperm from a donor.	☐	☐
ii) For artificial insemination to be successful the couple must still have sex.	☐	☐
iii) If a woman has low levels of FSH she would be given an ovary transplant.	☐	☐
iv) Women with no ovaries can receive an ovary transplant.	☐	☐
v) Women who can't produce eggs can have a baby using donated eggs.	☐	☐

b) Write out correct versions of the false statements below.

....

....

Q2 The **pill** is an **oral contraceptive** that contains oestrogen. Explain how it is used to reduce fertility.

....

....

....

Q3 Doctors can screen a foetus for **genetic diseases** before it's born by looking at its **DNA**.

a) Complete the following passage using the words provided.

needle   Down's Syndrome   fluid   amniocentesis   chromosomes

In ...., a long .... is used to remove some of the .... surrounding the foetus. This contains skin cells from the foetus and the .... in these can be analysed. This method can be used to identify conditions like ....

b) Explain why foetal screening raises ethical issues.

....

....

....

Controlling Fertility

Q4 Some couples who can't conceive naturally use **in vitro fertilisation (IVF)** to have a child.

a) Tick the box next to the correct description of IVF.

A man's sperm is placed into a woman's uterus.	☐
A healthy ovary is transplanted into a woman.	☐
A woman's eggs are fertilised outside of the body.	☐
A woman is injected with fertility hormones.	☐

b) Suggest one thing that needs to be healthy for IVF to be successful.

....

c) During a course of IVF treatment, **why** would a woman be given FSH injections?

....

d) What is meant by the term **surrogate mother** and when would one be used?

....

....

....

e) State the main risk associated with IVF.

....

f) Not all of the eggs that are fertilised are implanted into the woman's uterus.

i) What happens to the ones that are not implanted?

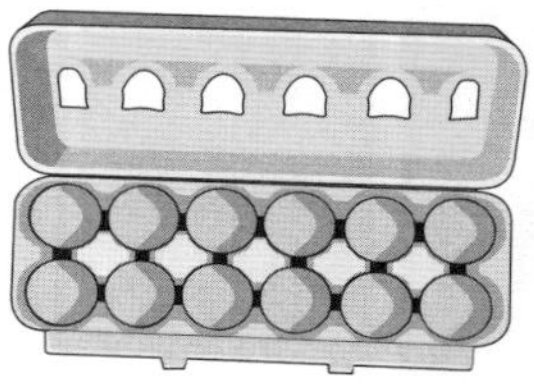

....

....

ii) Why do some people disagree with this?

....

g) Give **one** argument in favour of infertility treatments such as IVF.

....

More on Growth

Q1 Growth is stimulated by a hormone known as **growth hormone**.

a) Where in the body is growth hormone produced? Circle the correct answer.

pancreas **liver** **adrenal gland** **pituitary gland** **reproductive organs**

b) Fill in the missing words to complete the sentence below:

Human growth hormone stimulates general ....,
especially in the ....

Q2 Give two things that can cause extremes in human height.

1. ....

2. ....

Q3 Describe how **exercise** can influence growth.

....

....

Q4 A baby's growth was recorded. The results are shown on the **growth chart** below.

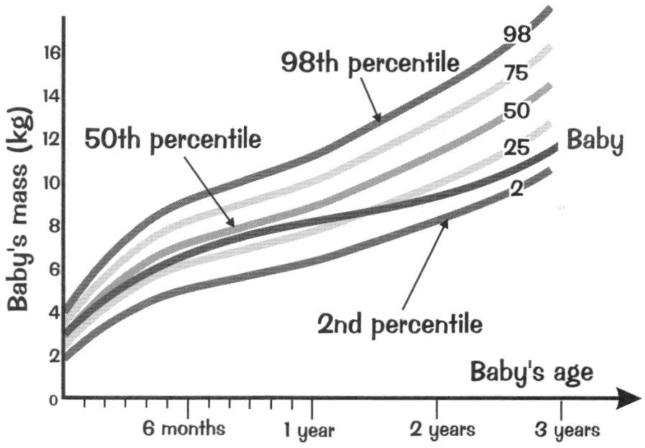

Would a doctor be concerned about the growth of this baby? Explain how you decided.

....

....

....

More on Growth

Q5 Over the past 100 years or so **life expectancy** in the UK has **increased** dramatically.

a) The boxes below contain changes that have occurred over this period and the result they have had. Match up the pairs by drawing a line between them.

People are financially better off

Previously fatal conditions can now be treated

Medical advances

Safer and healthier environment

Improved working and housing conditions

Healthier diet and lifestyle

b) State **two** problems associated with an increase in population.

....

....

Q6 Tick the boxes next to the statements to show whether they are **true** or **false**.

	True	False
a) All the parts of a foetus and baby grow at the same rate.	☐	☐
b) All the parts of a foetus grow at the same rate, but different parts of babies grow at different rates.	☐	☐
c) Different parts of a foetus and baby grow at different rates.	☐	☐

Q7 Zapphites have a similar growth pattern to humans. The graph shows the **head circumference** (size) of baby Zapphites between birth and 40 weeks. The shaded area shows where 90% of babies fall.

Baby's name	Age (weeks)	Head circumference (cm)
Charles	19	46.5
Edward	15	51
Engletree	34	54
George	27	49
Henry	23	49
Oliver	29	57
Richard	39	50
Xionbert	23	51.5

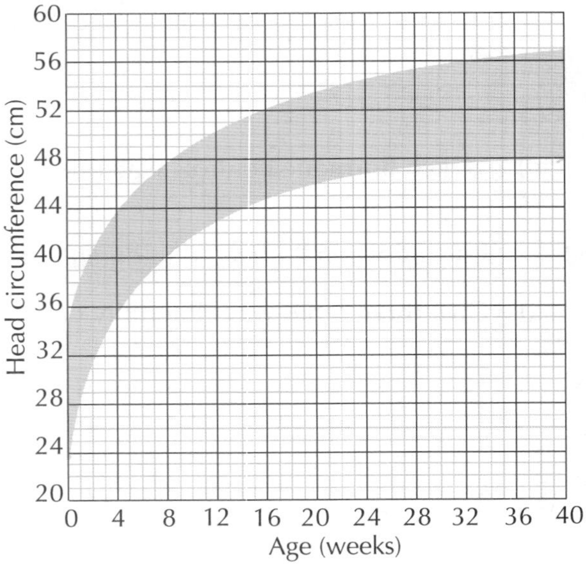

a) Plot the head circumferences of the above babies.

b) Which baby's head size may cause concern? ....

c) Why might Zapphite doctors monitor a baby's head circumference?

....

Zapphites come from the planet Zaphron.

Mixed Questions — Module B5

Q1 James was in a car crash and had a suspected **hip fracture**.

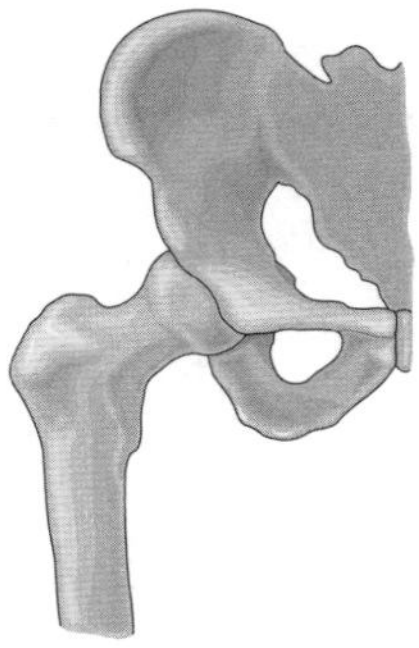

a) What **type** of joint is the hip joint?

....

b) What is the range of movement in this type of joint?

....

....

c) What holds the bones together at the joint?

....

d) James was taken to **surgery** to have the fracture pinned. He needs a **blood transfusion** whilst in surgery. He is blood group B. Which blood groups can he receive?

....

Q2 Your **heart rate** changes when you **exercise**.

a) Describe how your heart rate varies when you exercise.

....

b) Which **cells** control how fast the heart beats? ....

c) Exercise also affects how much **urine** you produce. Explain **why** it affects urine production.

....

....

d) Which **hormone** controls water reabsorption in the kidneys? ....

Q3 **Infertility** can be treated in different ways. A recently developed way is an **ovary transplant**.

a) Give **three** other ways infertility can be treated.

1. ....

2. ....

3. ....

b) To have an ovary transplant you need a **donated ovary**. The UK has a shortage of organ donors. Suggest how the organ donation system could be changed to increase the number of donors.

....

....

Mixed Questions — Module B5

Q4 The **kidneys** are responsible for **filtration** of the blood and **excretion** of waste from the body.

a) What are the three main roles that the kidneys perform?

1. ....

2. ....

3. ....

b) The table below shows the amounts of salt, sweat and urine lost by a particular person on a cold day, a hot day and a normal day. The same food and drink was consumed on each day and the same amount of exercise was done.

	salt in urine, g/day	salt in sweat, g/day	volume of urine, dm^3/day	volume of sweat, dm^3/day
cold day	3.1	2.0	2.8	0.2
hot day	4.6	3.1	2.0	2.3
normal day	3.5	2.5	2.1	1.1

i) In total, how much salt was lost on the cold day?

....

ii) Why is a greater volume of urine produced on a cold day than on a hot day?

....

....

c) If a person has kidney failure they are unable to filter their blood properly. One solution is a kidney transplant. Give **two** problems with organ transplants.

....

....

d) In addition to organs, blood can also be donated. Complete the table below to show which blood donors can give to which recipients.

Blood Group	Can give blood to	Can get blood from
A		
B		
AB		
O		

Think about the antigens on the surface of red blood cells

Mixed Questions — Module B5

Q5 A person's **lifestyle** choices can seriously affect their health.

a) Eating a lot of saturated fat can increase your risk of developing a **blocked coronary artery**. What happens when a coronary artery gets blocked?

....

b) Give two ways in which a doctor might investigate **heart function**.

1. .... 2. ....

c) Give an example of how **smoking** can affect the lungs.

....

d) Smoking can also decrease **lung capacity**. Lung capacity is measured using a **spirometer** which produces a **spirogram**.

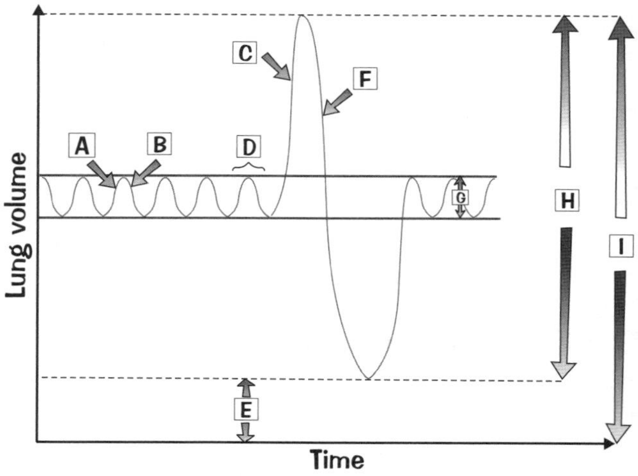

On the diagram, which letter corresponds to:

i) tidal air ....

ii) vital capacity ....

iii) one breath ....

iv) residual air ....

e) If a person's heart or lungs are damaged they can be replaced by donated organs. Describe two **ethical concerns** of organ donation.

1. ....

2. ....

Q6 The diagram represents the **menstrual cycle** in a particular woman.

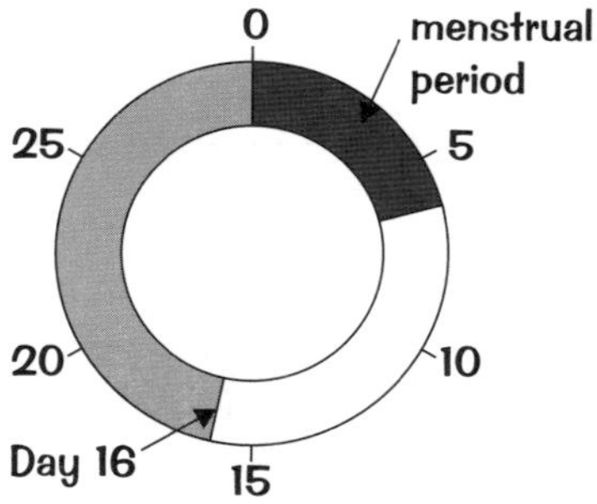

a) Oestrogen is one of the four main hormones that control the menstrual cycle. Give **two** functions of oestrogen.

....

....

b) Another key hormone in the menstrual cycle is FSH. Why is it unlikely that a woman with low levels of FSH will be able to get pregnant?

....

....

Bacteria

Q1 a) Draw lines to match up each **part** of a **bacterial cell** to its correct description.

DNA	maintains the cell's shape and helps to stop the cell from bursting
Flagellum	controls the cell's activities and replication
Cell wall	helps the cell to move

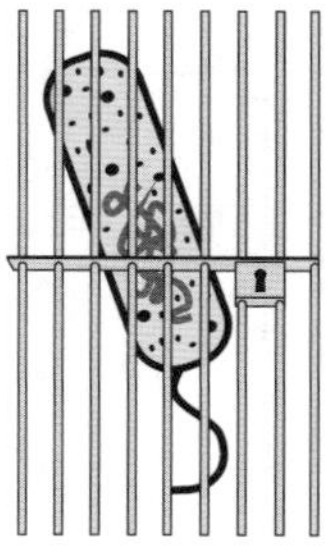

b) Some bacterial cells contain **plasmids**. What are plasmids?

....

Q2 Complete the passage below by choosing the correct word from each pair.

Bacteria are found in four main shapes — rods, curved rods, **spheres / cones** and spirals. They reproduce by a process called binary **fission / fusion**. This is a type of **asexual / sexual** reproduction, which basically means that each bacterial cell splits in **two / three**. In **cool / warm** conditions, with plenty of nutrients available, bacteria can reproduce very quickly.

Q3 Bacteria can survive in a huge range of **habitats**.

a) Suggest three different habitats that bacteria can survive in.

....

b) Explain why bacteria are able to live in such a wide range of habitats.

....

....

....

Top Tips: You can't really expect to pick up too many marks in this module if you don't know the basics, so make sure you're happy with these first few pages before you get stuck in to the rest. And trust me, these bacteria aren't all as scary as you might think. Some even make yoghurt...

Bacteria

Q4 Complete the passage about **yoghurt making** by filling in the gaps using the words below.

packaged **flavours** **pasteurised** **lactic acid** ***Lactobacillus*** **sterilised** **incubated**

First, all the equipment is .... to reduce the risk of contamination. Then, to make the yoghurt, milk is .... to kill off any unwanted microorganisms. A starter culture of .... bacteria is added and the mixture is .... The bacteria break down the lactose sugar into .... This causes the milk to clot and form yoghurt. .... (such as fruit) and colours can then be added and the yoghurt is ....

Q5 In suitable conditions, bacteria can reproduce very quickly.

a) Explain how storing food in a **fridge** can help to stop it **going off** so quickly.

....

....

b) Explain why many **illnesses** are caused by bacteria that reproduce very quickly.

....

....

Q6 Raymond is culturing bacteria from his kitchen sponge on an **agar plate**.

a) Explain why Raymond should use **aseptic technique** when he's culturing the bacteria.

....

....

b) Describe the **aseptic techniques** that Raymond should use as he works.

....

....

....

Microorganisms and Disease

Q1 a) Complete the diagram of a **virus** by filling in the missing labels.

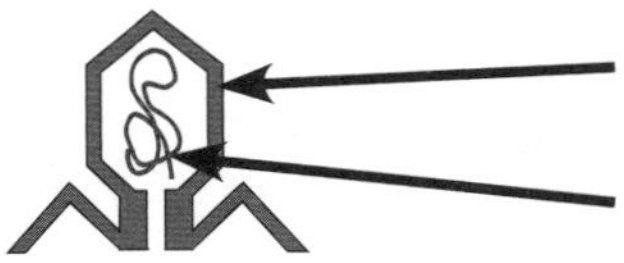

i) ....

ii) ....

b) In the spaces provided, write whether the following statements are **true** or **false**.

i) Viruses can only reproduce inside other living cells. ....

ii) A particular type of virus will only attack specific cells. ....

iii) Viruses only attack animal cells. ....

c) The diagram below shows how viruses reproduce. Add descriptions to each stage of the process.

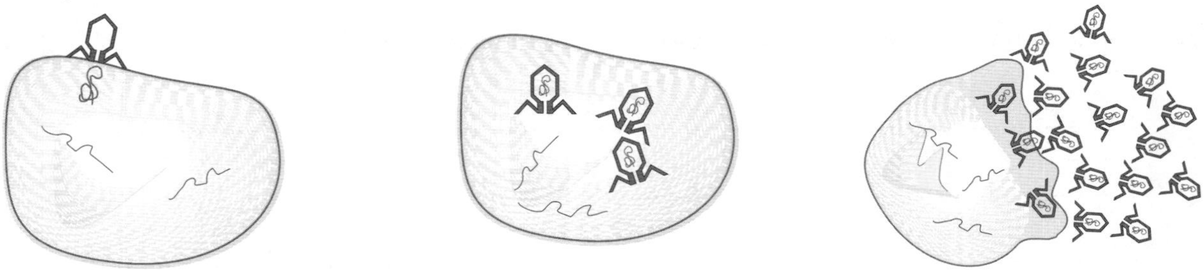

i) ....

....

ii) ....

....

iii) ....

....

Q2 For each of the three **diseases** below, draw lines to indicate how they are **spread** and give one **method of prevention** for each disease.

DISEASE	HOW IT'S SPREAD	METHOD OF PREVENTION
Influenza	Food	....
Cholera	Water	....
Food poisoning	Airborne droplets	....

Q3 Developing countries often have a **higher incidence of cholera** than developed countries. Explain fully why you think this might be.

....

....

....

Treating Infectious Diseases

Q1 Antiseptics and antibiotics are used to help control disease.

a) What type of microbes are **unaffected** by antibiotics? ....

b) Give **one** feature that antiseptics and antibiotics have in common.

....

c) Give **two** differences between antiseptics and antibiotics.

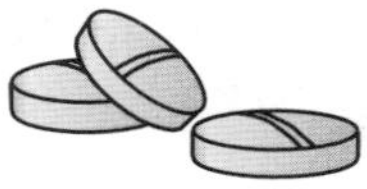

....

....

Q2 Explain what happens to **cause disease symptoms** once a microbe has entered the body.

....

....

....

Q3 There is concern about some bacteria developing resistance to antibiotics.

a) Put the stages in order (1-4) to show how a population of bacteria can develop **resistance** to a particular antibiotic through **natural selection**.

☐ The gene becomes more common in the population over time — giving the population resistance to the antibiotic.

☐ Bacteria with these mutated genes are more likely to survive and reproduce in a host being treated with the antibiotic.

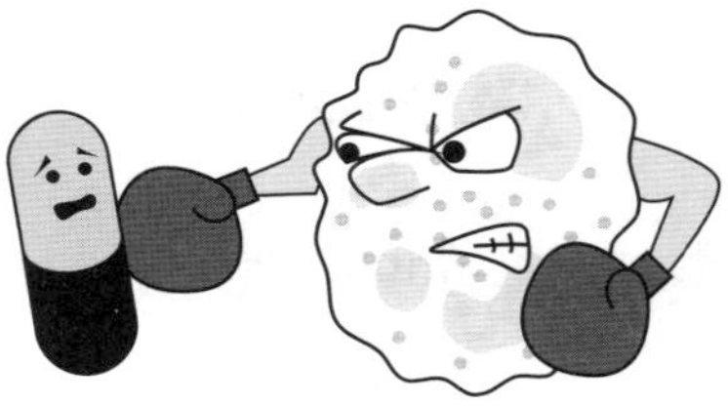

☐ Random mutations in bacterial DNA can lead to it being less affected by a particular antibiotic.

☐ The gene for antibiotic resistance will be passed on to lots of offspring.

b) i) Explain why doctors should **only prescribe** antibiotics when they're really **necessary**.

....

....

ii) State why it's always important to **complete a course** of antibiotics.

....

....

More on Infectious Diseases

Q1 Disease spreads rapidly after **natural disasters**.

Explain how each of the following can lead to ill health:

a) damaged sewage systems ....

....

b) damaged electrical supplies ....

....

c) displaced people ....

....

Q2 **Joseph Lister** and **Alexander Fleming** both made important contributions to **disease treatment**.

Decide whether the following statements about their work are **true** or **false**.

	Statement	True	False
a)	Joseph Lister discovered the antibiotic penicillin in 1928.	☐	☐
b)	Lister realised that infections of wounds were caused by microbes from the air.	☐	☐
c)	A mould called *Penicillium notatum* produced the first antibiotic to be discovered.	☐	☐
d)	The first antiseptic to be used was camomile acid.	☐	☐
e)	Penicillin was discovered by accident when bacteria contaminated a plate of mould.	☐	☐

Q3 **Louis Pasteur** did an experiment in which he boiled broth in **two different flasks** and allowed the broth to cool. Both **Flask 1** and **Flask 2** were open to the air, but **Flask 2** had a **long curved neck**.

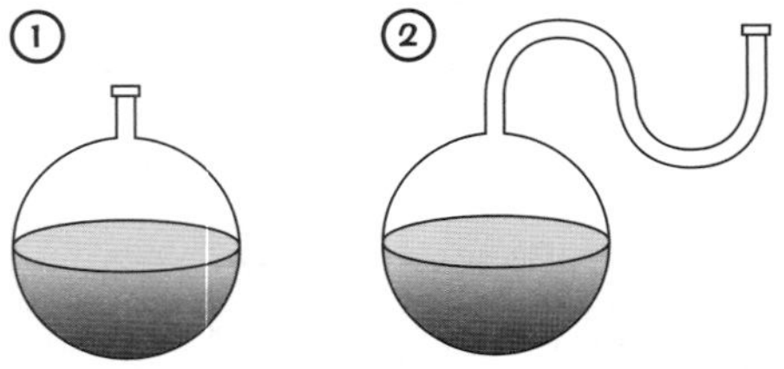

a) In which flask did the broth go bad, and why?

....

b) Explain why the broth in the other flask did not go bad.

....

c) In Pasteur's experiment, what is the purpose of Flask 1?

....

d) Suggest why Pasteur used a long curved neck for Flask 2, instead of sealing it with a stopper.

....

Yeast

Q1 a) Fill in the gaps to complete the symbol equation for anaerobic respiration in yeast.

$$C_6 \ldots\ldots_{12} \ldots\ldots_6 \rightarrow 2\ldots\ldots_2H_5OH + \ldots\ldots CO_2 \text{ (+ energy)}$$

b) Write out the **word equation** for this reaction in the space below.

....

c) Complete the following sentences by choosing the correct word from each pair.

In the absence of **oxygen / water**, yeast cells will respire **aerobically / anaerobically**.

This is known as **photosynthesis / fermentation**.

When **oxygen / water** is present they will respire **aerobically / anaerobically**.

Q2 The **growth rate** of yeast varies depending on the **conditions**.

a) Look at each of the graphs below and then choose the correct labels for the horizontal axes from the list provided.

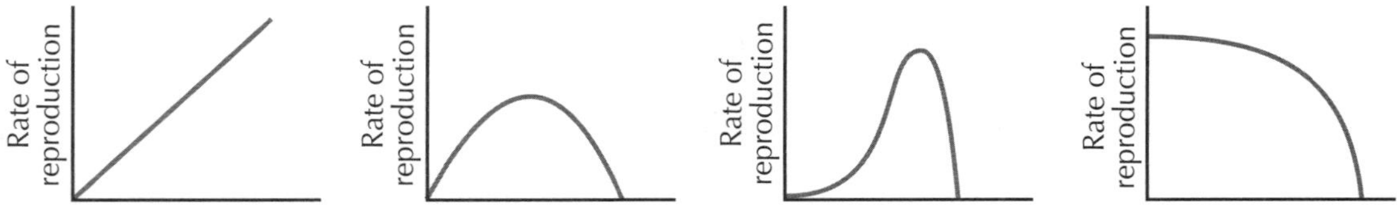

A B C D

Temperature	**Amount of food**	**Amount of toxic waste**	**pH**

A .... **B** ....

C .... **D** ....

b) Suggest one way of measuring how fast a culture of yeast is reproducing.

....

Q3 Some **food-processing factories** produce sugary waste that they need to get rid of.

a) Suggest why the waste water from these factories should not be dumped into rivers.

....

....

b) Explain why yeast can be used to treat the waste water before it is released.

....

Brewing

Q1 There are four main stages in making **beer**.

a) Number these stages from 1 to 4, where 1 is the first stage and 4 is the last.

☐ The beer is drawn off.

☐ Sugar is extracted from barley grains and hops are added.

☐ The beer is pasteurised.

☐ Yeast is added and the mixture is incubated.

b) Explain the purpose of adding yeast.

....

c) State **two** things that it's important to prevent from entering the fermentation vessels during fermentation.

....

d) Sometimes **clarifying agents** are added to the beer at the end of the brewing process. What effect do clarifying agents have on the beer?

....

Q2 **Ethanol** (alcohol) can be **toxic** to yeast cells.

Complete the following passage using the words from the boxes below.

decreases | increases | anaerobically | high | tolerate | kill

Some words can be used more than once.

As yeast cells respire ...., the concentration of ethanol in the fermentation mixture .... This eventually starts to .... the yeast cells. As the cells begin to die, the rate of fermentation .... Different species of yeast are able to .... different concentrations of ethanol. The species that can survive in .... ethanol concentrations can be used to produce strong wine and beer with a .... alcohol content.

Brewing

Q3 Give the meanings of the following words connected with **brewing**:

a) Fermentation ....

b) Distillation ....

c) Pasteurisation ....

Q4 The method used to make **wine** is similar to that used to brew beer.

a) Describe fully the process used to produce wine.

....

....

....

b) Beer is often pasteurised at the end of the brewing process, but wine is not.
Explain this difference.

....

....

....

Q5 **Distillation** can increase the alcohol content of fermented liquids.

a) Explain how this process happens.

....

....

....

b) Distillation is a commercial process. Where must it be carried out?

....

Top Tips: Beer and wine have been made for yonks — long before people understood that they were using the process of **anaerobic respiration** to turn sugars into alcohol. Not that they cared.

Biofuels

Q1 Complete the following passage about biomass using the words from the boxes below.

transformed	organic	biogas	bacteria	fermented	wood	energy

Biomass is .... material. The ....
stored in biomass can be .... into more useful forms in different ways. For example, ... from fast growing trees can be burnt as a fuel, releasing heat energy. Dead organic material can be .... by yeast or .... This process generates ...., which can also be burnt as a fuel.

Q2 **Biogas** is produced by certain kinds of **microorganisms** when they decompose waste matter.

a) Name the **two** gases that are the main components of biogas.

....

b) Name **three** other gases that are found in biogas in smaller amounts.

....

c) What can be the danger of using biogas that contains around 10% methane?

....

Q3 Biogas is used as **fuel**. Draw lines to match how the fuel is used, to what it powers or produces.

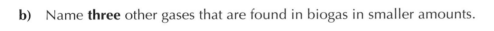

Biogas is burned to heat water	Generates electricity
Burned to drive an engine	Produces steam to heat central heating systems
Burned to power a turbine	Powers cars and buses

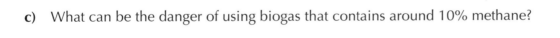

Biofuels

Q4 **Bacteria** are used to produce **methane**, a component of biogas.

a) Describe how several different types of bacteria are used in the production of biogas.

....

....

b) Describe how methane can be produced on a large scale.

....

....

....

Q5 An experiment was carried out to investigate the effect of **different temperatures** on **biogas production** in four digesters. The table below shows the results of these investigations.

TEMPERATURE	BIOGAS PRODUCTION (litres/hour)
15 °C	0.2
25 °C	3.1
35 °C	9.2
45 °C	0.0

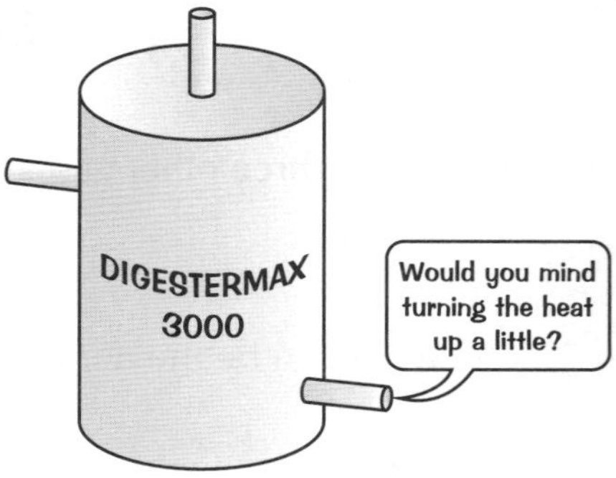

a) What was the best temperature for the production of biogas?

....

b) Suggest why more biogas was produced at this temperature than at any other temperature.

....

c) Suggest why biogas was **not** produced at 45 °C.

....

Top Tips: There's a lot to learn about biofuels — which is why there are a few more questions about them on the next page. Make sure you get to grips with this lot before turning over.

More on Biofuels

Q1 a) Write whether the following statements are **true** or **false**.

i) Biofuels are fossil fuels. ....

ii) Burning biogas doesn't produce particulates. ....

iii) Biogas isn't as 'clean' a fuel as diesel or petrol. ....

iv) Biogas contains less energy than natural gas. ....

b) Write a correct version of each false sentence in the space below.

....

....

Q2 Complete the passage below by circling the correct word(s) from each pair.

It's possible for biofuels to be produced and burnt without causing an overall increase in greenhouse gas levels. For this to happen, biofuels need to be burnt at the same **rate** / **temperature** that the biomass is produced and the plants need to be grown on land that **has** / **hasn't** been cleared by burning other vegetation.

Q3 Apart from an increase in greenhouse gas levels, give two possible **environmental problems** that can result from large areas of land being cleared to produce **biofuels**.

1. ....

2. ....

Q4 **Gasohol** is another **alternative fuel** which is widely used in some parts of the world.

a) Describe the composition of gasohol.

....

b) Give one use of gasohol. ....

c) Name one country where gasohol is used on a large scale. ....

d) The use of gasohol is only **economically viable** in areas with **small oil reserves**. What else does an area need to make the use of gasohol economically viable?

....

Soils

Q1 The diagrams below show the particles in three different soil types — **sand**, **clay** and **loam**.

a) Label each soil type in the spaces provided.

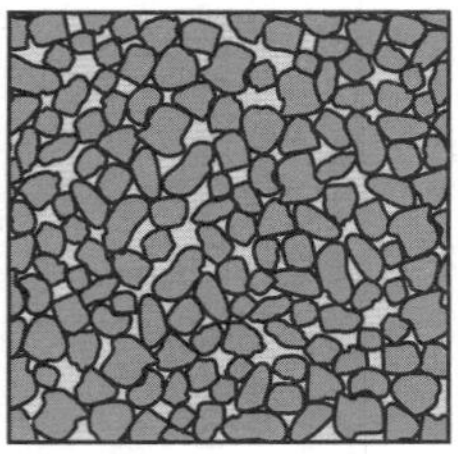

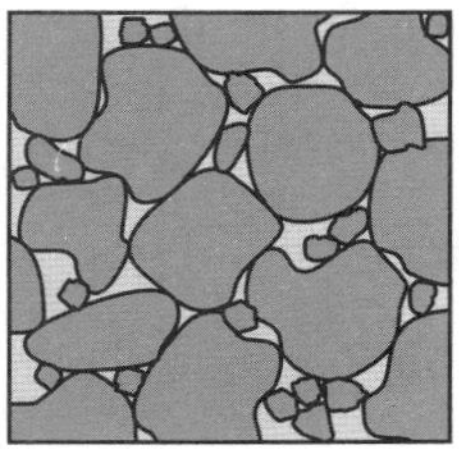

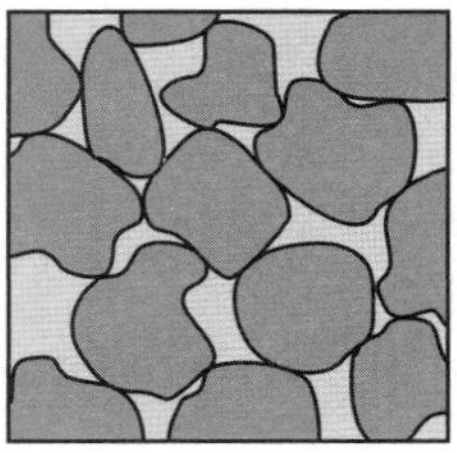

i) .... **ii)** .... **iii)** ....

b) **Clay soils** have a relatively low air content. Explain why this is in terms of **soil particle size**.

....

....

c) Most soils also contain **humus**. What is humus?

....

Q2 Darren has collected two samples of soil — one from his neighbour's vegetable patch, and one from his own vegetable patch. He wants to compare the **water content** of the two soil samples.

a) Describe how Darren might measure the water content of each soil sample.

....

....

....

....

b) The soil from Darren's vegetable patch is a sandy soil. His neighbour's soil is a clay soil. Which of these soils will have larger particles?

....

c) Explain how the particle size will affect the water content of the two soils.

....

....

Life in the Soil

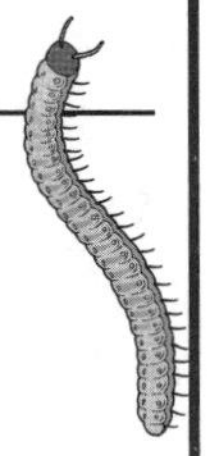

Q1 The diagram shows a food web from the soil in Nelson's garden.

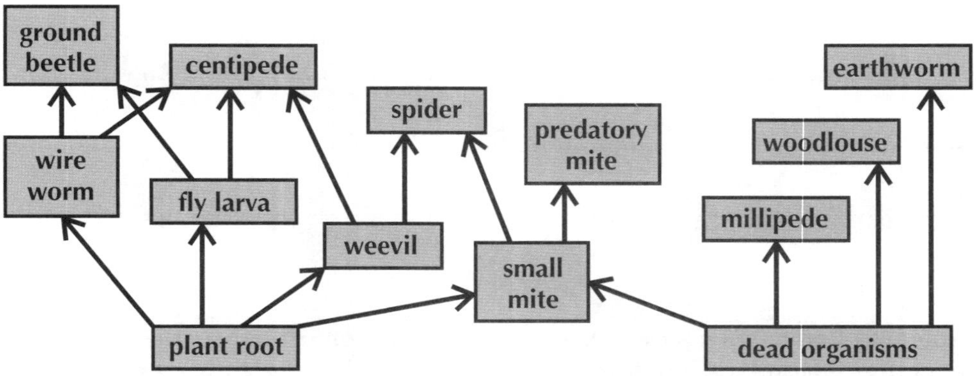

Nelson applied a pesticide to the soil which killed all the woodlice.
Explain how this may affect the following organisms:

a) Small mites ....

....

b) Wire worms ....

....

Q2 Explain why **humus** is important to life in the soil.

....

....

Q3 Complete the following passage about **earthworms**, using the words in the box below.

aeration	neutralise	Darwin	layers	nutrients	fertile	drainage	oxygen

Charles .... was one of the first people to discover why earthworms are so good for soil structure and fertility. One reason is that the worms' burrows allow air to enter the soil. This is called .... and it provides organisms in the soil with .... The burrows also increase ...., which prevents soil becoming waterlogged. Worm droppings help to .... soil acidity, making the soil more .... Their activities also help to mix up the soil ...., distributing .... more evenly.

Life in Water

Q1 Life in water and life on land are very different.
Give two **advantages** and two **disadvantages** of living in water.

....

....

....

Q2 Most species of crab, such as **spider crabs**, live in **water**. Other species, such as **robber crabs**, live on **land** and will actually drown if dropped into water.

Which species of crab — the spider crab or the robber crab — is likely to be more tolerant of changes in temperature? Give a reason for your answer.

....

....

Q3 Many **plants** that grow on land have **tough woody parts**.
Suggest why few plants found in **water** have woody parts.

Woody parts provide the plant with support.

....

Q4 The **Amoeba** is a single-celled organism that is found in **fresh water**. The solute concentration in an amoeba cell is **higher** than that of the surrounding water.

a) Suggest why the Amoeba tends to absorb too much water.

....

....

b) Explain the role of the contractile vacuole in preventing the Amoeba cells bursting.

....

....

c) Related species of single-celled organism living in the sea don't have a vacuole.
Suggest why not.

....

....

More on Life in Water

Q1 Nigel works for the **Environment Agency**. He's investigating reports that a **stream** (which runs alongside a farmer's land) has become covered in a thick blanket of **algae**.

a) What **substance** used in agriculture could be the cause of this algal growth?

....

b) i) Put the following sentences in order to describe the problems that rapid algal growth will cause.

- ☐ **Animals are unable to respire and die.**
- ☐ **Algae die and decay.**
- ☐ **Decomposers feed on dead algae.**
- ☐ **All the oxygen in the water is used up.**

ii) Name the **process** that causes rapid algal growth. ....

Q2 **Phytoplankton populations** can increase in ponds during the summer months.

a) Explain why phytoplankton populations usually increase in the summer and not the winter.

....

b) What effect will an increase in the phytoplankton population have on the zooplankton in the pond? Explain your answer.

....

Q3 State **three** possible **water pollutants**.

....

Q4 Complete the passage below about **photosynthesis in water** by filling in the missing words.

Photosynthesis is affected by temperature, ... intensity and the availability of minerals. These factors change in different .... and at different depths. In winter and in deep water, light intensity and temperature are ...., so they limit the rate of photosynthesis. In the summer when .... and light intensity are ...., mineral concentration is much .... — so mineral concentration limits the amount of photosynthesis.

More on Life in Water

Q5 **Phytoplankton** are often the producers in ocean food webs.

a) Name another type of organism that often acts as a producer in **deep-sea** food webs.

....

b) Some deep-sea food webs rely on '**marine snow**' as a source of nutrients. What is 'marine snow'?

....

Q6 An investigation was carried out into the number of bacteria found along a stream. A **sewage outflow pipe** was located midway along the study site. The graph shows the number of bacteria found.

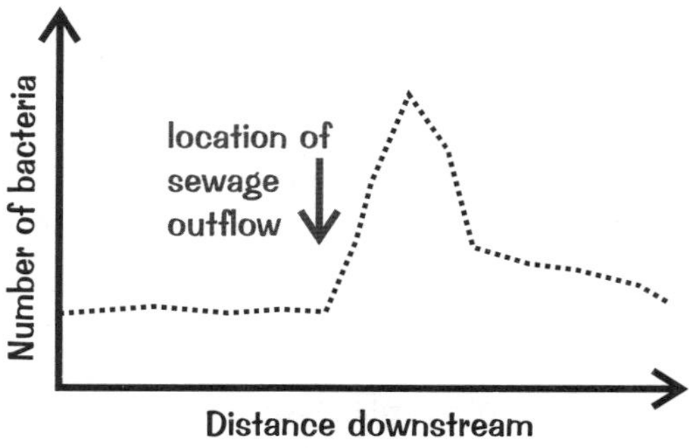

Explain the changes in levels of bacteria at increasing distance downstream from the outflow pipe.

....

....

Q7 **DDT** is a chemical that has been used as a **pesticide** to kill insects such as mosquitoes and lice.

a) Explain why DDT is passed along food chains.

....

....

b) Which organisms in a food chain are most likely to be poisoned by DDT? Explain your answer.

....

....

c) Name another chemical that can accumulate in food chains in the same way.

....

Enzymes in Action

Q1 **Biological washing powders** contain enzymes. One example is the **protease enzyme**.

a) Explain why protease enzymes are added to biological washing powders.

....

b) Name **two** other enzymes that can be added to biological washing powders and describe the function of each.

....

....

c) Explain why it is easier to remove stains once they have been digested by enzymes.

....

....

Q2 Andrea buys a new brand of **biological washing powder**. When she tries it out she finds it doesn't work as well as the non-biological washing powder she used to use. She decides this is because her tap water is **too alkaline**.

a) Explain why a biological washing powder might not work very well in alkaline tap water.

....

b) Andrea's dad thinks the washing powder would work better if she used a cooler wash cycle. Explain why biological washing powders work best at **moderate temperatures**.

....

Q3 Explain the role of the enzyme **invertase** in the **food industry**.

....

....

....

Top Tips: There are loads of different enzymes and we have loads of different uses for them — they've a role in everything from washing clothes to making food taste better. Remember though, all enzymes have a few things in common — and that includes being sensitive to temperature and pH.

More Enzymes in Action

Q1 Enzymes can be **immobilised** using various methods.

a) Describe how enzymes can be immobilised in **alginate beads**.

....

....

b) Circle two **advantages** of using immobilised enzymes from the list below.

Immobilised enzymes can be used in continuous flow processes.

Immobilised enzymes always work faster than normal enzymes.

Immobilised enzymes can be found naturally.

Immobilised enzymes don't contaminate the product.

Q2 Test strips used for detecting the presence of **glucose** in **blood** contain immobilised enzymes. When exposed to glucose in a blood sample, they cause a colour change at the tip of the strip. Suggest why **immobilised** enzymes are used.

....

....

Q3 Some people are **lactose intolerant**. They can only eat **dairy products** that have been treated to remove the **lactose** (milk sugar).

a) Explain why lactose intolerant people can't eat dairy products that contain lactose.

....

b) Describe what would happen if a lactose intolerant person drank milk containing lactose.

....

c) Describe how **immobilised enzymes** are used to produce lactose-free milk.

....

....

....

More on Genetic Engineering

Q1 What is a **transgenic organism**? Circle the correct definition from the options below.

A genetically modified organism

An organism that can't reproduce

An organism that reproduces asexually

A physically modified organism

Q2 Explain how it's possible for genes from one organism to function in another organism.

....

....

Q3 Bacteria can be genetically engineered to produce **human insulin**. Complete the passage below by circling the correct word(s) from each pair to explain how this is done.

First, scientists must identify the gene that controls insulin production in humans. The gene is cut from the DNA with **restriction** / **ligase** enzymes, leaving **sticky** / **blunt** ends. A bacterial **plasmid** / **cell** is then cut open using the same enzymes. **Restriction** / **ligase** enzymes are used to join the ends of the insulin gene and the bacterial DNA together. The plasmid now contains the insulin **molecule** / **gene** and is taken up by bacteria. The bacteria reproduce rapidly, quickly resulting in millions of cells that can produce **ligase** / **human insulin**.

Q4 Plasmids are often used as **vectors** in genetic engineering.
Explain what is meant by the term 'vector'.

....

Q5 Describe the role of **assaying techniques** in genetic engineering.

....

....

DNA Fingerprinting

Q1 Circle the correct word(s) to complete each of the following sentences about DNA fingerprinting.

a) Before DNA fingerprinting can start, the DNA must be **extracted** / **replicated**.

b) The DNA sample is broken down into fragments using restriction **acids** / **enzymes**.

c) DNA fragments are separated using **electric current** / **photographic film**.

d) Larger DNA fragments **move further than** / **don't move as far as** smaller DNA fragments.

e) DNA will show up on photographic film if it's been marked by a **radioactive probe** / **chemical stain**.

Q2 Choose from the words below to complete the passage about the **DNA fingerprinting** process.

positive   negatively   bigger   electrophoresis
smaller   positively   suspended   negative   separated

After the DNA has been cut into fragments, these fragments are .... using a process called .... They're .... in a gel, and an electric current is passed through the gel. DNA is .... charged, so it moves towards the .... electrode (anode). .... bits travel faster than .... bits, so they move further through the gel.

Q3 The following **DNA samples** are being used in a **murder investigation**. The DNA samples are from the victim, three suspects and some blood which was found on the victim's shirt.

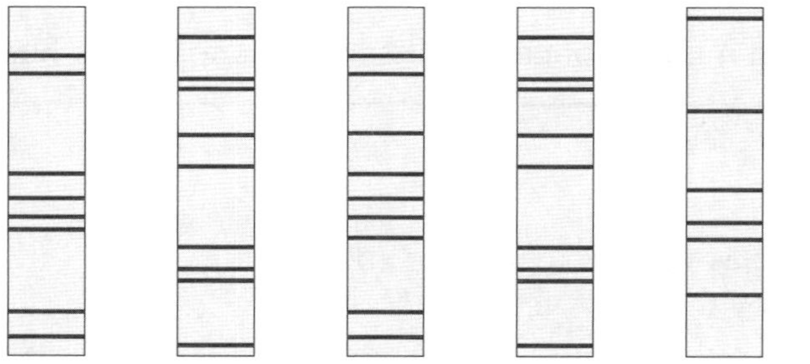

a) Which two individuals are likely to be **related** to each other? Explain your choice.

....

b) Who is the most likely culprit based on the DNA evidence? Explain your answer.

....

DNA Fingerprinting

Q4 Put the following stages of **DNA fingerprinting** into the correct order.

Compare the unique patterns of DNA.

Separate the sections of DNA.

Extract the DNA from the cells.

Cut the DNA into small sections.

1. ....

2. ....

3. ....

4. ....

Q5 A thoroughbred horse breeder has collected DNA samples from each of her horses. Her **new foal's DNA** is **sample 1**. The **mother** of the foal is **sample 2**. Study the **DNA profiles** and complete the table showing which horse is the **foal's father**.

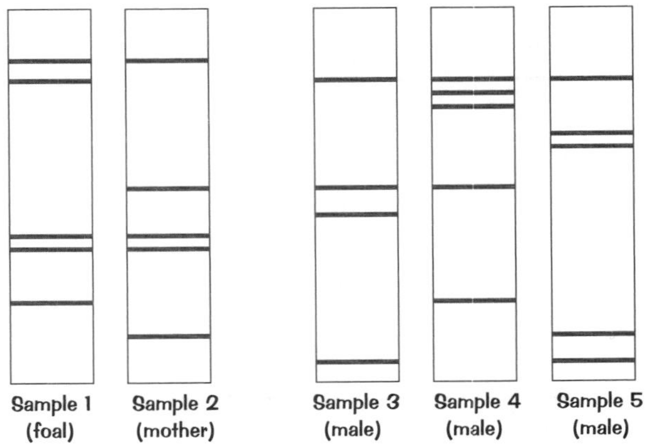

	Foal	Mother	Father
DNA sample	Sample 1	Sample 2	

Q6 A national **genetic database** would allow everyone's unique pattern of DNA to be saved on file.

a) Give one use of a national genetic database.

....

b) Give one drawback of a national genetic database.

....

Mixed Questions — Module B6

Q1 **Influenza** (flu) can be a fatal disease.

a) **i)** Name the type of microorganism that causes influenza.

....

ii) Describe the structure of this type of microorganism.

....

b) Explain why doctors shouldn't prescribe antibiotics to treat influenza.

....

Q2 The quality of the crops farmers grow is affected by the soil in their fields.

a) Why are earthworms beneficial to farmers with acidic soils?

....

b) Farmers often use fertilisers to improve the quality of their soil. Unfortunately, these fertilisers can cause eutrophication if they get into waterways. In the box below draw a flow diagram showing how fertilisers getting into water can lead to fish dying.

Q3 Some scientists are studying a species of shrimp that is very sensitive to **pH**. The shrimp is found in lakes with a pH **above 7.0**.

a) Name **one** other property of water that can be monitored by indicator species.

....

b) Describe how the scientists could use the shrimp as an **indicator species** for pH in other lakes.

....

....

Mixed Questions — Module B6

Q4 The rate at which **yeast** reproduces can be changed by controlling the conditions in which the yeast is growing.

a) Complete the following statements by circling the correct word from each pair.

i) Yeast reproduces **faster** / **slower** when oxygen is present.

ii) Yeast reproduces **faster** / **slower** with increasing temperature, until the **minimum** / **optimum** is reached.

iii) Before the **minimum** / **optimum** is reached, growth rate roughly **doubles** / **trebles** for every 10 °C rise in temperature.

b) Does yeast respire aerobically or anaerobically in the production of beer?

....

c) Write a balanced equation for the respiration of yeast in beer production.

....

Q5 a) Fill in the missing labels on the diagrams to show the main components of **biogas** and **gasohol**.

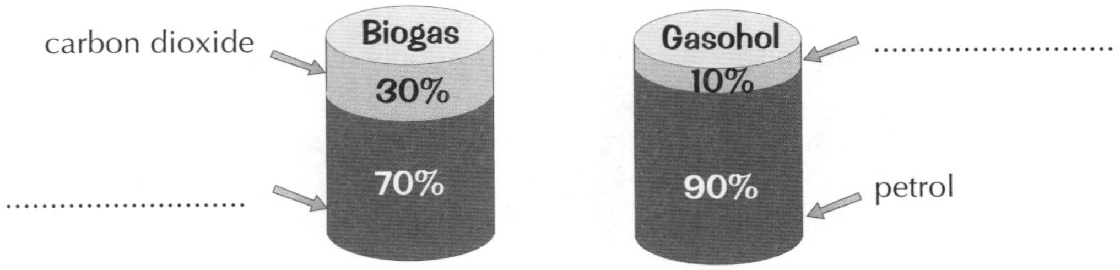

b) Suggest why it's important to monitor the level of the main component in **biogas**.

....

....

c) Give **three** uses of biogas.

....

d) Currently, most biogas is produced at around 35 °C. If the bacteria that produce the gas could be modified to produce biogas more efficiently at lower temperatures then biogas could be produced in cooler parts of the world.
Outline the stages that would be involved in modifying bacteria so that they respire more effectively at cooler temperatures if a suitable gene has been found in another organism.

....

....

....

Mixed Questions — Module B6

Q6 The soil in Zele's garden is described as a **loam soil**.

a) What is a 'loam soil'?

....

....

b) Zele is interested in the air content of his soil and decides to carry out an experiment to measure it. Describe an experiment that Zele could carry out to measure the air content of his soil.

....

....

....

....

c) **i)** The air content of a soil is important because many soil organisms depend on a good supply of **oxygen**. Explain why this is the case.

....

ii) Explain why soil organisms also depend on a supply of **water**.

....

Q7 Abigail studies food webs in the ocean.

a) Some of the food webs Abigail studies are **grazing food webs**. Explain what is meant by the term 'grazing food web'.

....

....

b) **i)** Suggest why **phytoplankton** are not found in deep-sea food webs.

....

ii) What type of organisms can act as producers in these deep-sea ecosystems?

....

c) Name **one** other source of nutrients in deep sea ecosystems.

....

Atoms, Molecules and Compounds

Q1 Complete the passage below by circling the correct word in each pair.

> If an atom loses one or more electrons it becomes **positively** / **negatively** charged. If an atom gains one or more electrons it becomes **positively** / **negatively** charged. Charged atoms are known as **ions** / **molecules**.

Q2 Draw lines to match up the following substances with their formulas. You won't need to use all of the formulas.

substance	formula
hydrochloric acid	$MgCO_3$
calcium carbonate	H_2SO_4
sulfuric acid	$PbNO_3$
magnesium sulfate	HNO_3
	$CaCO_3$
	$MgSO_4$
	HCl

Q3 The diagram below shows the displayed formula of 1-chloropentan-3-ol.

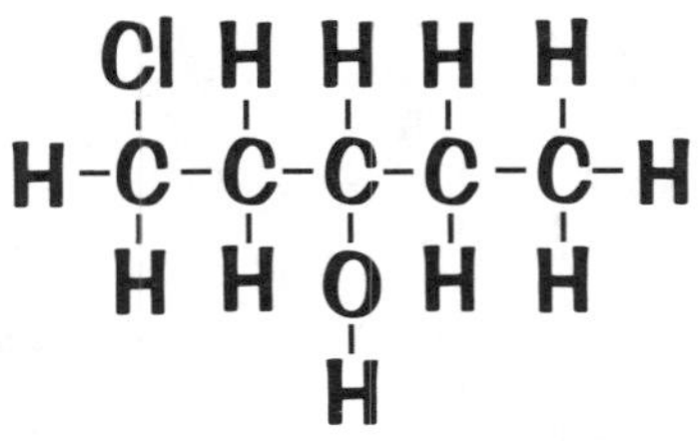

a) Describe what a displayed formula shows.

....

....

....

b) Write down the molecular formula of 1-chloropentan-3-ol.

....

....

Q4 Briefly describe how ionic and covalent bonds are formed.

ionic: ....

covalent: ....

__Chemical Equations__

Q1 Balance these equations.

a) H_2SO_4 + Fe → $Fe_2(SO_4)_3$ + H_2

b) Cu + O_2 → CuO

c) $Ba(OH)_2$ + H_3PO_4 → $BaHPO_4$ + H_2O

Not all of the lines will need numbers on.

d) Fe + Cl_2 → $FeCl_3$

e) Ag_2O → Ag + O_2

f) Na + O_2 → Na_2O_2

Q2 The diagram below shows the displayed formula for heptanoic acid.

$$H-\overset{\overset{\displaystyle H}{|}}{\underset{\underset{\displaystyle H}{|}}{C}}-\overset{\overset{\displaystyle H}{|}}{\underset{\underset{\displaystyle H}{|}}{C}}-\overset{\overset{\displaystyle H}{|}}{\underset{\underset{\displaystyle H}{|}}{C}}-\overset{\overset{\displaystyle H}{|}}{\underset{\underset{\displaystyle H}{|}}{C}}-\overset{\overset{\displaystyle H}{|}}{\underset{\underset{\displaystyle H}{|}}{C}}-\overset{\overset{\displaystyle H}{|}}{\underset{\underset{\displaystyle H}{|}}{C}}-\overset{\overset{\displaystyle O}{\|}}{C}-OH$$

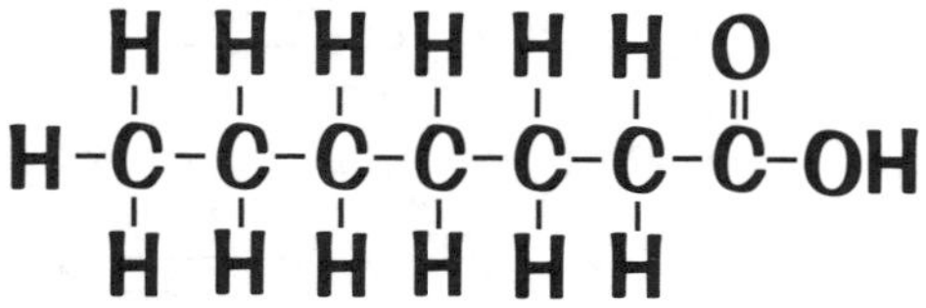

A chemist reacts heptanoic acid with oxygen to give carbon dioxide and water.

a) Write down the word equation for this reaction.

..

b) Write down the molecular formula for heptanoic acid.

..

Q3 The evil Professor Jewitt has stolen your lunch money and is holding it to ransom. He says he will return the lunch money if you can balance the fiendishly difficult chemical equation below in less than 2 minutes.

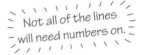

Balance the equation below to retain your dignity and win back your lunch money.

.... NH_4F + NaOH + $Al(OH)_3$ →

.... Na_3AlF_6 + H_3N + H_2O

The Mole

Q1 a) **Complete** the following sentence.

> One mole of atoms or molecules of any substance will have a .... in grams equal to the .... for that substance.

b) What is the molar mass of each of the following?

Use a periodic table to help you. There's one at the front of this book.

i) C_2H_5OH ....

ii) $Cu(OH)_2$ ....

c) What is the mass of each of the following?

i) 2 moles of nitric acid, HNO_3. ....

ii) 0.5 moles of calcium carbonate, $CaCO_3$. ....

iii) 5.4 moles of magnesium hydroxide, $Mg(OH)_2$. ....

Q2 What is the **relative atomic mass** of an element?

....

....

Q3 a) Write down the formula for calculating the **number of moles in a given mass**.

....

b) How many **moles** are there in each of the following?

i) 54 g of aluminium, Al.

....

ii) 112 g of sulfur dioxide, SO_2.

....

iii) 198.75 g of copper oxide, CuO.

....

Q4 Calculate the **mass** of each of the following.

a) Magnesium in 0.75 moles of magnesium oxide, MgO.

....

b) Chlorine in 0.025 moles of lead chloride, $PbCl_2$.

....

Reacting Masses and Empirical Formulas

Q1 Use **atomic masses** to calculate the percentage by mass of the following elements in their compounds.

a) Cu in $CuSO_4$

....

b) C in C_5H_{10}

....

c) O in H_2O

....

Q2 Calculate the percentage by mass of an element using the following **experimental data**.

a) There is 5.48 g of H in 21.92 g of CH_4.

....

b) There is 13.44 g of C in 49.28 g of CO_2.

....

c) There is 57.6 g of S in 176.4 g of H_2SO_4.

....

d) There is 64.35 g of K in 166.65 g of KNO_3.

....

Q3 The equation below shows lead nitrate reacting with sodium chloride to form lead chloride and sodium nitrate.

$$Pb(NO_3)_2 + 2NaCl \rightarrow PbCl_2 + 2NaNO_3$$

Calculate the mass of lead chloride ($PbCl_2$) that is produced when 40.95 g of sodium chloride (NaCl) is used in the reaction.

....

....

....

Top Tips: When you're doing these types of questions remember to use your periodic table to find the all the atomic masses of the elements. Otherwise you might end up with the wrong numbers and that'll make all your calculations all higgledy piggledy, which is never a nice thing.

Reacting Masses and Empirical Formulas

Q4 The reaction between calcium carbonate and hydrochloric acid is shown below.

$$CaCO_3 + 2HCl \rightarrow CaCl_2 + CO_2 + H_2O$$

Calculate the mass of calcium carbonate ($CaCO_3$) that is required to produce 83.25 g of calcium chloride ($CaCl_2$).

....

....

....

Q5 Give the **empirical formula** for each of the following compounds.

a) $C_2H_4O_2$ .... **b)** C_4H_8 .... **c)** P_4O_{10} ....

Q6 Calculate the **empirical formula** of the compound formed when:

a) 20 g of calcium combines with 8 g of oxygen.

....

....

b) 5.4 g of aluminium combines with 9.6 g of sulfur.

....

....

Q7 An **oxide** of **sulfur** contains **60% oxygen**.

a) What is the percentage of sulfur in the oxide?

....

b) Calculate the empirical formula of the oxide.

....

....

Q8 A **carbonate** was found to contain **28.6% magnesium**, **14.3% carbon** and **57.1% oxygen**. Work out the **empirical formula** of the compound.

....

....

....

Concentration

Q1 a) Circle the correct word below to complete the following sentence.

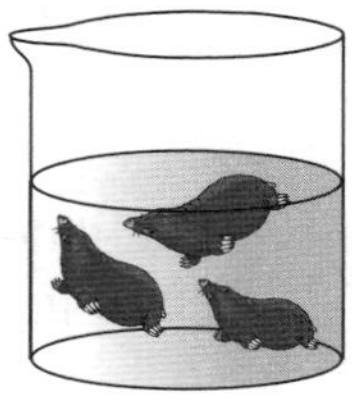

> The more solute you dissolve in a given volume, the **more** / **less** crowded the solute molecules are and the **more** / **less** concentrated the solution.

b) Write down the formula for calculating the number of moles in a solution.

....

c) Use the formula to calculate the number of moles in:

i) 50 cm^3 of a 2 mol/dm^3 solution. ....

ii) 250 cm^3 of a 0.5 mol/dm^3 solution. ....

iii) 550 cm^3 of a 1.75 mol/dm^3 solution. ....

d) **200 cm^3** of a solution contains **0.25 moles** of iron hydroxide, $Fe(OH)_3$.
Calculate its **molar concentration**.

....

e) What **volume** of a 1.6 mol/dm^3 solution of calcium hydroxide contains **2 moles** of calcium hydroxide?

....

Q2 Calculate the concentration of these solutions:

a) 4 moles of sodium chloride in 800 cm^3

....

b) 0.69 moles of sodium hydrogencarbonate in 300 cm^3

....

Q3 Cedric is testing substance X as a new **drug** for asthma. The drug is manufactured at a concentration of **1 mol/dm^3** and is then **diluted** before being given to patients.

He calculates that a patient taking part in the trial should take **250 ml** of a **0.2 mol/dm^3** solution of substance X each day. Describe how he could make up this strength solution.

....

....

....

....

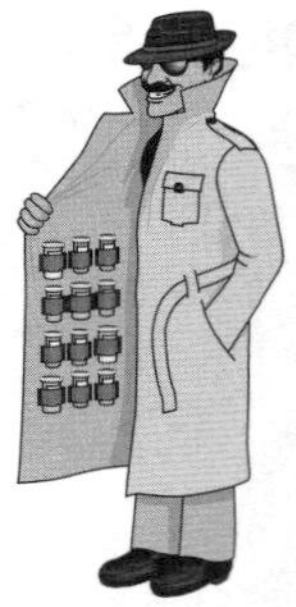

Concentration

Q4 Calculate the volume of a **5.6 g/dm³** KOH solution that contains **0.5 moles**.

Hint: convert the concentration to mol/dm³ first.

....

....

....

Q5 Calculate the volume of a **223.3 g/dm³** $CuSO_4$ solution that contains **0.7 moles**.

....

....

....

Q6 Jared has a solution of dipotassium phosphate buffer with a concentration of **0.75 mol/dm³**.

a) Calculate how many moles are in 100 ml of this solution.

....

....

b) Jared wants to make 150 ml of 0.1 mol/dm³ dipotassium phosphate.
Describe how he could dilute the solution he has to make the new solution.

....

....

....

Q7 Heather needs to produce **200 cm³** of **0.1 mol/dm³** hydrochloric acid solution for an experiment. She has been provided with a **2 mol/dm³** hydrochloric acid solution and some water.

Describe how Heather could make the required solution.

....

....

....

Concentration

Q8 **'Froggart's'** blackcurrant cordial is **diluted** before drinking. Its contents are summarised on the label, as shown.

> **Froggart's blackcurrant cordial**
> **Contains real fruit juice!**
> **Dilute using 1 part cordial to 5 parts water.**
> **100 ml diluted cordial contains:**
> **8 mg vitamin C (20% GDA)**
> **10.6 g sugar**
> **Trace of sodium & protein**
> **189 kJ energy**

a) **i)** What do the letters GDA stand for?

ii) What does the GDA tell you?

b) **i)** Donald pours 50 ml of cordial. How much water should he add?

ii) What percentage of the GDA of vitamin C will this volume of cordial provide?

Work out the volume of diluted cordial first.

c) What volume of diluted cordial would provide 100% of the GDA of vitamin C?

Q9 The **nutritional information** on the label of some vegetable stock powder is shown below.

	g per 100 g stock powder	g per 250 ml serving
protein	10.5	0.5
carbohydrate	29.4	1.5
fat	8.1	0.4
fibre	0.7	0.04
sodium	17.6	0.9

a) 150 g of powder will make 7.5 litres of stock. What volume will 100 g of powder make?

b) Show that the mass of sodium given for a 250 ml serving agrees with that given for 100 g of powder.

c) Sodium is present mainly as sodium chloride (salt).
How much sodium chloride will 100 g of stock powder contain?

d) Suggest why this is probably an overestimate of the amount of salt in the stock powder.

Titrations

Q1 Describe the method for carrying out an acid/alkali titration. Include the names of any equipment that you would use.

....

....

....

....

....

Q2 An **indicator** is used to determine the **end-point** of a titration.

a) Complete the following table to show the colour of the indicators in different solutions.

Indicator	Colour in strong acid solutions	Colour in strong alkali solutions
phenolphthalein		
litmus		

b) Explain why universal indicator is **not** a suitable indicator to use in an acid-base titration.

....

....

Q3 Sophie wanted to find out the volume of an acidic solution required to neutralise 25 cm^3 of an alkaline solution. She did a rough titration first, then four more titrations. Her results are shown in the table.

Titration	Volume of acid added / cm^3
1	16.0
2	15.4
3	17.6
4	15.3
5	15.5

a) Why did Sophie carry out a rough titration at the beginning?

....

....

b) Which value is anomalous? ....

c) What is the advantage of carrying out the titration several times?

....

d) Calculate the average volume of acid needed to neutralise 25 cm^3 of the alkaline solution.

....

Titrations

Q4 The graph shows the **pH curve** from a titration.

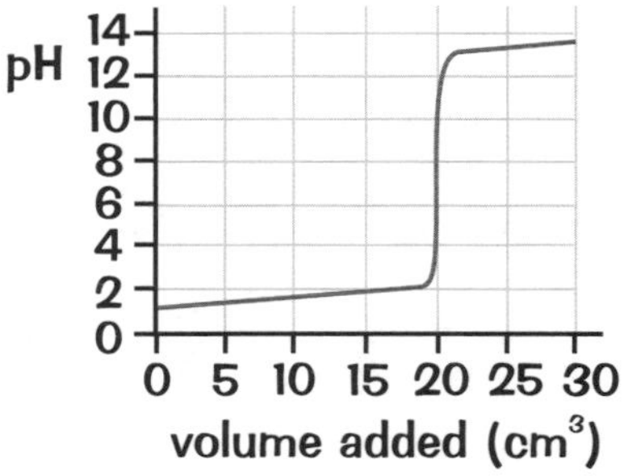

a) Does this pH curve show an acid being added to an alkali or an alkali being added to an acid?

....

b) How is the end-point of a titration illustrated on a pH curve?

....

....

c) What volume of alkali is needed to neutralise the acid? ....

Q5 Anna carried out a titration in which **hydrochloric acid** was gradually added to **10 cm^3** of calcium hydroxide solution in a conical flask. The results are shown in the table.

Volume of HCl (cm^3)	pH
0	11.0
2	10.6
4	10.1
5	6.0
6	2.0
8	1.4
10	1.1

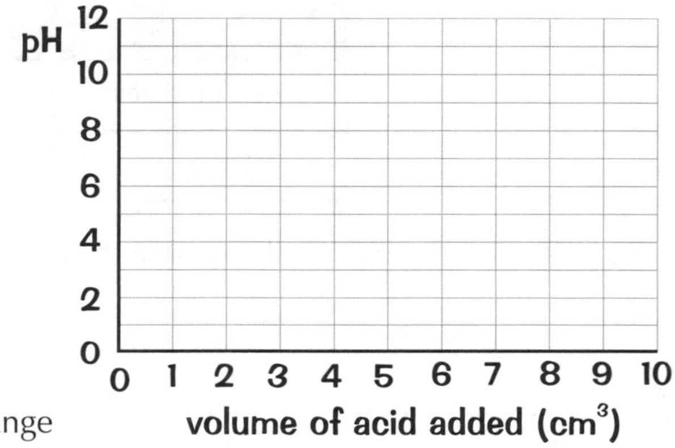

a) Plot a graph on the grid provided to show the change in pH as the titration proceeds. Draw a 'best fit' curve.

b) Estimate the pH after 7 cm^3 of acid has been added. ....

c) What volume of acid was needed to neutralise the alkali? ....

Q6 **20 cm^3** of a **sodium hydroxide** solution was titrated with **0.1 mol/dm^3 hydrochloric acid**. **10 cm^3** of hydrochloric acid was needed to neutralise the alkali. Calculate the concentration of the sodium hydroxide solution using the steps below.

a) How many moles of hydrochloric acid were needed to neutralise the alkali?

....

b) 1 mole of HCl neutralises 1 mole of NaOH. How many moles of sodium hydroxide reacted?

....

c) Calculate the concentration of the sodium hydroxide. Give your answer in mol/dm^3.

....

Titrations

Q7 Alex wanted to analyse the concentration of **phosphoric acid** in different brands of cola drinks. He allowed the carbon dioxide to escape from the drinks and titrated **20 cm³** of each drink using **0.01 mol/dm³ sodium hydroxide solution**. He used a pH meter to measure the pH.

The results are shown in the graphs opposite.

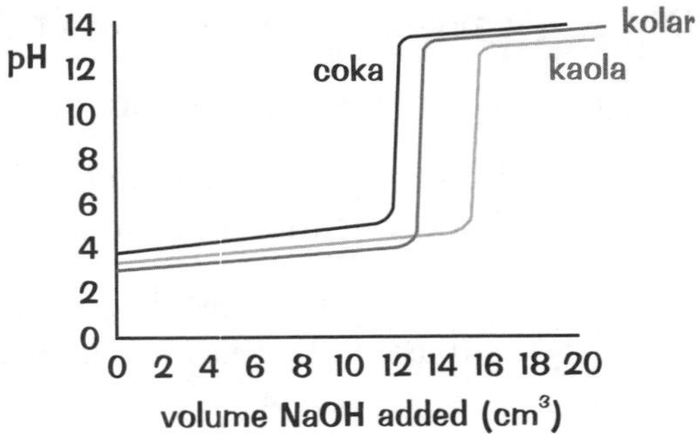

a) Suggest why Alex did not use an indicator to measure pH.

....

b) Suggest why Alex allowed the carbon dioxide to escape before analysing the drinks.

CO_2 in water gives carbonic acid.

....

....

c) Which drink had the greatest phosphoric acid concentration? ....

Q8 In a titration, **12.5 cm³** of **0.04 mol/dm³ calcium hydroxide** solution was needed to neutralise **25 cm³** of **sulfuric acid**. Calculate the **concentration** of the sulfuric acid in mol/dm³.

$$H_2SO_4 + Ca(OH)_2 \rightarrow CaSO_4 + 2H_2O$$

....

....

....

Q9 In a titration, **10 cm³** of **hydrochloric acid solution** was used to neutralise **30 cm³** of **0.1 mol/dm³ potassium hydroxide solution**.

$$HCl + KOH \rightarrow KCl + H_2O$$

What was the concentration of the hydrochloric acid in mol/dm³?

....

....

....

Top Tips: Aargh, calculations. As if Chemistry wasn't tricky enough without maths getting involved too (but at least it's not as bad as Physics). Actually, these aren't the worst calculations as long as you tackle them in stages and know your equations.

Gas Volumes

Q1 Complete the sentences by circling one answer in each pair.

a) Gas syringes can measure the **volume** / **area** of gas accurate to the nearest **dm^2** / **cm^3**.

b) A burette is **more** / **less** accurate for measuring the volume of gas collected than a measuring cylinder because the graduations on a burette are to the nearest **0.1 cm^3** / **10 cm^3**.

c) A balance can be used to measure the **volume** / **mass** of gas released in a reaction. The mass of the reactants **increases** / **decreases** as the reaction proceeds.

Q2 Choose the **most suitable method**, from A to D, for the tasks below. (Use each method once only.)

A — Bubble the gas into an upside-down gas jar filled with water.

B — Attach the conical flask to an empty boiling tube.

C — Bubble the gas into an upside-down burette filled with water.

D — Attach the conical flask to a gas syringe.

Sulfur dioxide and ammonia are soluble in water.

a) **Collecting** and **measuring** ammonia gas. ....

b) **Collecting** and **measuring** oxygen. ....

c) **Collecting** hydrogen. ....

d) **Collecting** sulfur dioxide. ....

Q3 a) What is the **volume** of **one mole** of any gas at room temperature and pressure? Circle your answer.

24 dm^3 **12 dm^3** **2.4 dm^3** **36 dm^3**

b) What volume is occupied by the following gases at room temperature and pressure?

i) 0.5 moles of hydrogen chloride. ....

ii) 6.25 moles of ammonia. ....

c) How many moles are there in the following gases at room temperature and pressure?

i) 240 cm^3 of hydrogen. ....

ii) 8 dm^3 of chlorine. ....

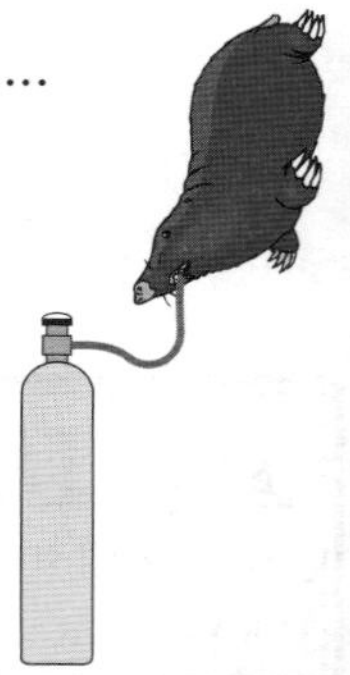

Following Reactions

Q1 Use the words provided to complete the passage below.

new	gas	highest	faster	reaction	reactants	slower	limiting

You can tell that a chemical .... is taking place if a ....
substance is forming. You may see a colour change, a precipitate forming or a
.... being given off. Reactions are .... at the start
because this is when the reactants are at their .... concentrations.
Eventually the reaction gets ...., and it stops when one of the
.... is used up. This is called the .... reactant.

Q2 Tim adds a large piece of **magnesium** to some dilute **hydrochloric acid** and records the total volume of hydrogen gas produced every 10 seconds. His results are shown in the graph below.

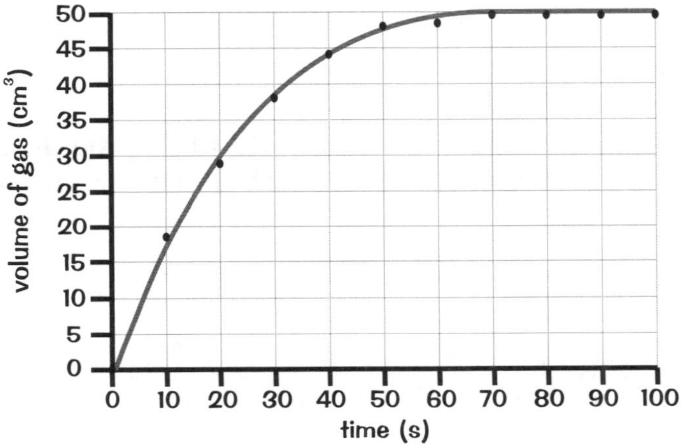

a) Use the graph to answer the following questions.

i) How long did it take for the reaction to stop? ....

ii) How much hydrogen was produced in total? ....

iii) How much gas had been formed by 25 seconds? ....

iv) How long did it take to produce 25 cm^3 of hydrogen gas? ....

b) At the end of the reaction Tim noticed that a very small piece of **magnesium** was left in the flask. Which of the reactants is the limiting reactant?

....

c) Circle the correct answer to the following questions.

i) If the amount of limiting reactant is halved, the total volume of hydrogen produced is:

25 cm^3 50 cm^3 75 cm^3 100 cm^3

ii) If the amount of limiting reactant is doubled, the total volume of hydrogen produced is:

25 cm^3 50 cm^3 100 cm^3 Not possible to predict.

Following Reactions

Q3 The graph shows the results of a reaction carried out under three different sets of **conditions**.

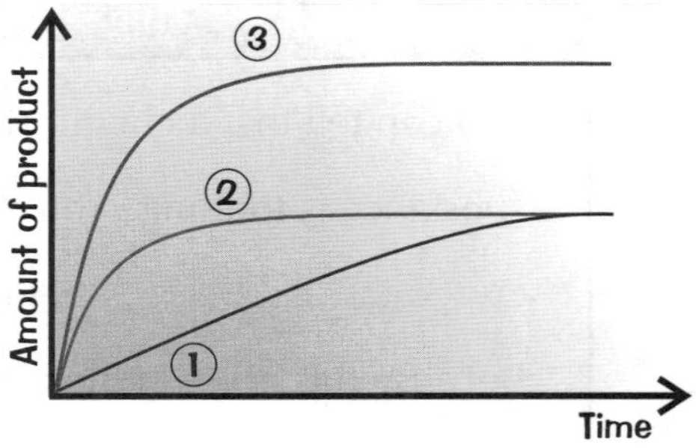

a) State which reaction has the largest amount of limiting reactant. ....

b) Explain in terms of particles why the amount of product produced is directly proportional to the amount of limiting reactant.

....

....

....

c) Reaction 2 and 3 both stop before reaction 1. Explain why a reaction stops after a period of time.

....

Q4 The graph below shows the results of a reaction between **10 g** of **marble chips** and **25 cm³** of **0.5 mol/dm³ hydrochloric acid**. (The acid is the limiting reactant.)

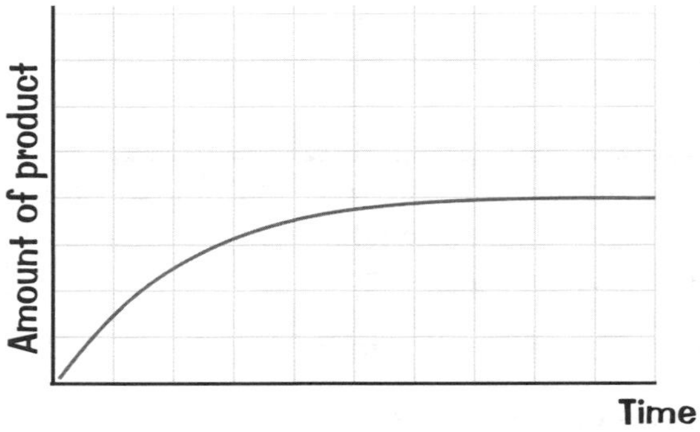

For each of the following reactions, sketch and label a curve of the reaction on the graph above and explain why you have drawn that particular curve. (The acid is the limiting reactant in all the reactions.)

a) **Reaction 1** — 10 g of marble chips with 25 cm³ of 1.0 mol/dm³ hydrochloric acid.

....

b) **Reaction 2** — 10 g of marble chips with 12.5 cm³ of 1.0 mol/dm³ hydrochloric acid.

....

Top Tips: If you can't read graphs and tables, you'll struggle with questions about following reactions. Never fear though — all it takes is practice and you'll be an expert. Bored, but an expert.

Equilibrium

Q1 Use words from the list below to complete the following passage.

reversible	decrease	equilibrium	faster	increase	escape	
reactants	closed	products	react	equal	slower	concentrations

A reaction that can go in both directions is called a .... reaction. This means that the .... of the reaction can themselves .... to give the original .... To reach equilibrium, the reaction must happen in a .... system where products and reactants can't ....

As the reactants react their concentrations will ...., so the forward reaction will get .... At the same time, the concentration of the products will ...., which makes the backward reaction get .... When the rate of the forward and backward reaction are ...., the reaction has reached an .... and the .... of the reactants and the products do not change.

Q2 Look at this diagram of a **reversible reaction**.

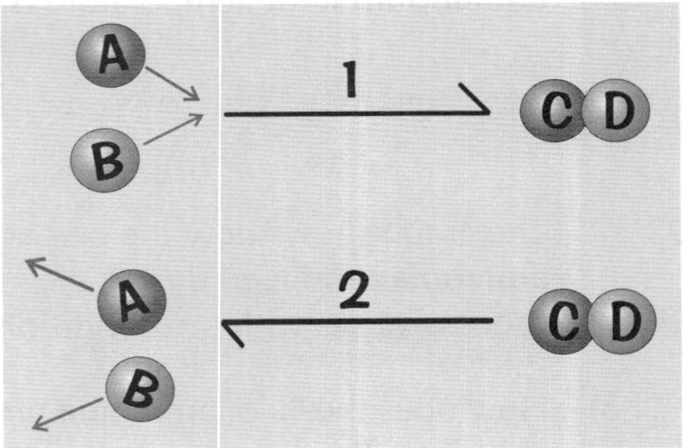

a) For the forward reaction:

i) Give the reactant(s). ....

ii) Give the product(s). ....

b) Write the equation for this reversible reaction.

....

c) Name **three** things that can change the position of an equilibrium.

....

d) State whether the concentration of the reactants will be higher, lower or the same as the concentration of the products when the position of the equilibrium is:

i) on the left. ....

ii) on the right. ....

iii) at equilibrium. ....

Changing Equilibrium

Q1 Write the letter of one equation, A to C, to which the following statements apply.

A $N_2O_4(g) \rightleftharpoons 2NO_2(g)$

B $2SO_2(g) + O_2(g) \rightleftharpoons 2SO_3(g)$

C $H_2(g) + I_2(g) \rightleftharpoons 2HI(g)$

a) A change in pressure has no effect on the position of equilibrium. ....

b) An increase in pressure moves the equilibrium to the left. ....

c) An increase in pressure moves the equilibrium to the right. ....

Q2 Substances A and B react to produce substances C and D in a reversible reaction.

$$2A(g) + B(g) \rightleftharpoons 2C(g) + D(g)$$

a) Tick the box to show which direction the equilibrium will move when the amount of one of the substances is changed.

	Left	Right
i) Amount of A increased.	☐	☐
ii) Amount of B reduced.	☐	☐
iii) Amount of C reduced.	☐	☐
iv) Amount of D increased.	☐	☐

b) The forward reaction is **exothermic**. What will happen to the amount of the reactants at equilibrium if the temperature is increased?

....

Q3 The graph shows how the percentage of **ammonia** produced during the Haber process varies with the **conditions**.

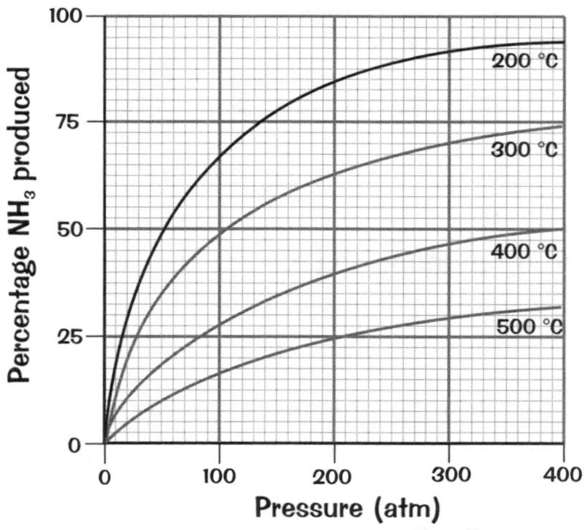

a) How does the % of ammonia produced change as the **pressure increases**?

....

b) How does the % of ammonia produced change as the **temperature increases**?

....

c) Explain, using the data from the graph, whether the reaction is exothermic or endothermic.

....

....

Changing Equilibrium

Q4 **Ethanol** is produced from **ethene** and **steam**. The equation for the reaction is given below.

$$C_2H_4(g) + H_2O(g) \rightleftharpoons C_2H_5OH(g)$$

The table shows how the percentage of ethanol at equilibrium changes as the pressure changes (at a fixed temperature).

Pressure (atm)	20	30	40	50	60	70	80	90	100
% ethanol at equilibrium	20	24	28	32	38	43	48	54	59

a) How many molecules are there on the left-hand side of the equation? ....

b) What happens to the amount of **reactants** at equilibrium when the pressure is increased?

....

c) Explain what happens to the percentage of ethanol at equilibrium when the pressure **decreases**.

....

....

Q5 For each of the following reactions, describe what would happen to the **position** of the equilibrium if the **temperature** and **pressure** of the mixture were **increased**.

a) $H_2(g) + Cl_2(g) \rightleftharpoons 2HCl(g)$ (forward reaction is exothermic)

Temperature ....

Pressure ....

b) $4NH_3(g) + 5O_2(g) \rightleftharpoons 4NO(g) + 6H_2O(g)$ (forward reaction is exothermic)

Temperature ....

Pressure ....

c) $N_2O_4(g) \rightleftharpoons 2NO_2(g)$ (forward reaction is endothermic)

Temperature ....

Pressure ....

d) $2SO_2(g) + O_2(g) \rightleftharpoons 2SO_3(g)$ (forward reaction is exothermic)

Temperature ....

Pressure ....

The Contact Process

Q1 Complete the following sentences by circling the correct word(s) in each pair.

The **reduction** / **oxidation** of sulfur dioxide to sulfur trioxide is **not reversible** / **reversible**, and the reaction is **exothermic** / **endothermic**.

When the temperature is increased, you get **more** / **less** sulfur trioxide, as the position of equilibrium is pushed to the **left** / **right**.

If the temperature of any reaction is increased, the rate of the reaction **decreases** / **increases** because the particles have **more** / **less** energy.

A **compromise** / **maximum possible** temperature of **350 °C** / **450 °C** gives quite a high yield of sulfur trioxide, but produces it quite **slowly** / **quickly**.

Q2 **Complete** and **balance** the following equation involved in the Contact Process.

$$\ldots\ldots\ldots\ldots + \ldots\ldots\ldots\ldots \rightleftharpoons \ldots\ldots\ldots\ldots SO_3$$

Q3 The Contact Process uses **atmospheric pressure** to make sulfur trioxide.

a) Explain what happens to the yield of sulfur trioxide when the pressure is increased.

....

....

....

b) Give **two** reasons why the Contact Process is carried out at atmospheric pressure.

....

....

Q4 The Contact Process uses a catalyst.

a) State the catalyst that is used in the Contact Process.

....

b) Describe the effect of the catalyst on:

i) the rate of the reaction.

....

ii) the position of the equilibrium.

....

Strong and Weak Acids

Q1 Tick the correct boxes to show whether the following statements are **true** or **false**.

		True	False
a)	Strong acids always have higher concentrations than weak acids.	☐	☐
b)	Strong acids ionise completely in water.	☐	☐
c)	Nitric acid ionises only very slightly in water.	☐	☐
d)	Ionisation of weak acids is reversible.	☐	☐
e)	Weak acids don't form an equilibrium mixture in water.	☐	☐

Q2 Strong and weak acids react with **reactive metals** and with **carbonates** in the same way.

a) Complete the following sentences by circling the correct word(s) in each pair.

i) Hydrochloric acid and ethanoic acid react with magnesium to give **hydrogen** / **oxygen**.

ii) Hydrochloric acid and ethanoic acid react with calcium carbonate to give **carbon dioxide** / **carbon monoxide**.

b) i) Do strong acids react **faster** or **slower** than weak acids? ....

ii) Explain your answer. ....

....

....

Q3 Fill in this table by completing the equations showing the **ionisation** of these acids, with the correct **reaction symbol**, and stating whether the acid is **strong** or **weak**.

Name	Equation	Strong / Weak
Nitric acid	HNO_3 $\rightarrow$ .... + ...	....
Benzoic acid	C_6H_5COOH $\rightleftharpoons$ .... + ...	....
Hydrobromic acid	HBr .... + ...	Strong
Formic acid	HCOOH .... + ...	Weak

Top Tips: Strong and weak acids are similar but different, and it's all down to how much they ionise. If you know that weak acids only ionise a bit, all the rest pretty much follows on from there.

Strong and Weak Acids

Q4 The graph shows the results of a reaction between an excess of **magnesium** and **50 cm³ of 0.2 mol/dm³ hydrochloric acid**.

For each of the following reactions, sketch a curve on the graph above. (All of the reactions stop once the acid has run out.)

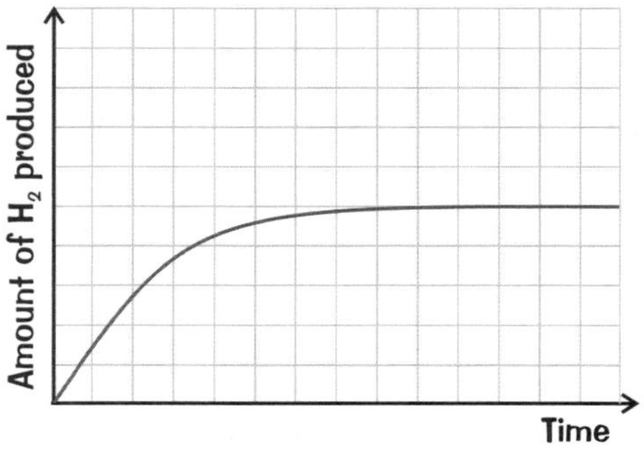

a) **Reaction 1** — Excess magnesium is reacted with 50 cm^3 of 0.4 mol/dm^3 hydrochloric acid.

b) **Reaction 2** — Excess magnesium is reacted with 50 cm^3 of 0.2 mol/dm^3 ethanoic acid.

Q5 Strong acids can be dilute and weak acids can be concentrated. Describe the difference between acid **strength** and acid **concentration**.

....

....

....

Q6 Write **equations** to show the **ionisation** of the following acids.

a) Hydrochloric acid (HCl) ....

b) Ethanoic acid (CH_3COOH) ....

Q7 Fred does an experiment to show that hydrochloric acid reacts faster than ethanoic acid with **magnesium ribbon**.

What difference would you expect to see in the amount of gas Fred collected after:

a) both acids had reacted for 20 seconds?

....

b) both acids had reacted completely?

....

Strong and Weak Acids

Q8 The graph below shows the volume of CO_2 released when calcium carbonate was added to flasks containing **nitric acid** or **ethanoic acid**. Both acid solutions were at the same concentration.

a) State which of the acid solutions will have a higher concentration of H^+ ions. Explain your answer.

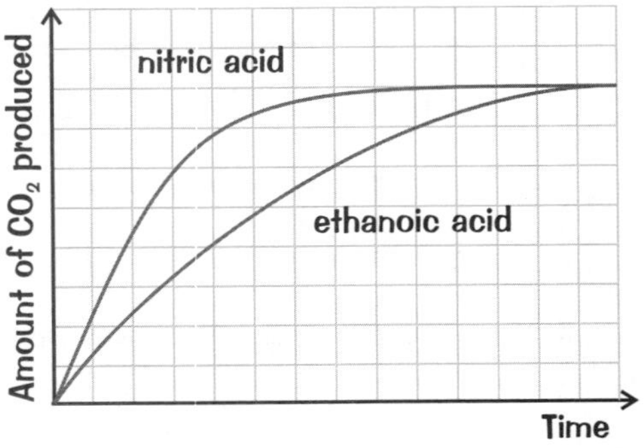

....

....

....

....

b) Explain in terms of collision frequency why the reaction between calcium carbonate and ethanoic acid is slower than the reaction between calcium carbonate and nitric acid.

....

....

....

Q9 Explain the following:

a) The pH of nitric acid (a strong acid) is lower than the pH of lactic acid (a weak acid) (of the same concentration).

....

....

b) Hydrochloric acid is a better electrical conductor than ethanoic acid (of the same concentration).

....

....

c) Weak acids and strong acids of the same concentration will produce the same amount of product.

....

....

....

d) Electrolysis of both hydrochloric acid and ethanoic acid will produce hydrogen.

....

....

Precipitation Reactions

Q1 Look at the **equations** below, then complete the sentences by circling one answer in each pair.

barium nitrate	+	potassium sulfate	$\rightleftharpoons$	barium sulfate	+	potassium nitrate
$Ba(NO_3)_2(aq)$	+	$K_2SO_4(aq)$	$\rightleftharpoons$	$BaSO_4(s)$	+	$2KNO_3(aq)$

a) The precipitate formed is **$BaSO_4$** / **KNO_3**. This is shown by the state symbol **aq** / **s**.

b) The **potassium** / **barium** ions are spectator ions — they're **involved** / **not involved** in the reaction.

c) The ionic equation only involves the ions that **remain in solution** / **precipitate out**.

d) The reaction is **fast** / **slow** because of the **large** / **small** number of collisions.

Q2 Complete the table below to show the ionic equation and the colour of precipitate that forms when halide ions react with **Pb^{2+}** ions from lead nitrate.

Halide ion	Ionic equation	Colour of precipitate
Cl^-		
I^-		
Br^-		

Don't forget to include state symbols in your reactions.

Q3 Jason has been given a solid sample which he suspects is **magnesium sulfate** ($MgSO_4$).

a) Describe a method Jason could use to show that the compound contains sulfate ions.

b) What is the positive result of the test described in part **a)**?

c) Write the word equation for this reaction.

Q4 Explain why **ionic substances** in precipitation reactions must be **in solution**.

Preparing Insoluble Salts

Q1 **Lead(II) nitrate** was reacted with **potassium iodide** to give an insoluble salt.

a) Which of the following is the correctly balanced symbol equation for this reaction? Tick one box.

A $PbNO_3(aq) + KI(aq) \rightarrow PbI_2(aq) + 2KNO_3(aq)$ ☐

B $Pb(NO_3)_2(aq) + 2KI(aq) \rightarrow PbI_2(s) + 2KNO_3(aq)$ ☐

C $Pb(NO_3)_2(aq) + 2KI(s) \rightarrow PbI_2(aq) + 2KNO_3(s)$ ☐

D $Pb(NO_3)_2(s) + 2KI(aq) \rightarrow PbI_2(s) + 2KNO_3(aq)$ ☐

b) Name the **insoluble salt** formed. ....

Q2 Louise wants to prepare the insoluble salt **barium sulfate**. She starts by making two solutions, one of barium nitrate and one of copper(II) sulfate.

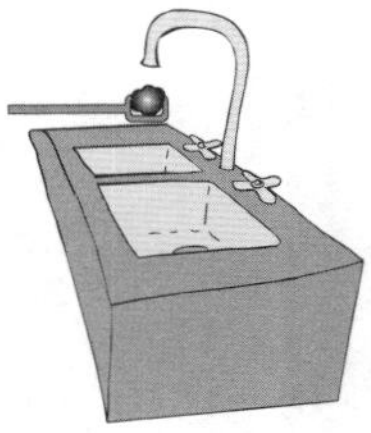

a) Louise uses tap water to dissolve the solids.
What would be a better choice, and why?

....

b) Complete the balanced symbol equation (including state symbols) for this reaction.

$$Ba(NO_3)_{2\,(aq)} + CuSO_{4\,(aq)} \rightarrow \text{.................................} + \text{.................................}$$

c) Describe the method used to produce the insoluble salt.

Stage 1.

....

....

Stage 2.

....

....

Stage 3.

....

....

Top Tips: The process for making an insoluble salt is always the same. So it doesn't matter what reactants they give you — the method will be the same. That makes life a lot easier.

Mixed Questions — Module C5

Q1 There are two common oxides of chromium, **oxide V** and **oxide W**.

a) 5.2 g of chromium reacted with 2.4 g of oxygen to produce oxide V.
Calculate the empirical formula of oxide V.

....

b) Oxide W has a percentage composition by mass of 52% chromium and 48% oxygen.
Work out its empirical formula.

....

Q2 During the Contact Process, **sulfur dioxide** reacts with **oxygen** to form **sulfur trioxide**.

a) Write down the balanced symbol equation for this reaction.

....

b) **i)** Is this reaction exothermic or endothermic? ....

ii) Would high or low temperatures favour a high rate of reaction? ....

c) **i)** How many moles of reactant react to produce two moles of product? ....

ii) Would high or low pressures favour a high yield of product? ....

d) **i)** What are the actual industrial conditions used during the production of sulfur trioxide?

....

ii) Why are these a compromise? ....

....

....

Q3 Simon wants to know if an unknown solution contains a **halogen**.

a) Describe a test that Simon could do to show if halide ions are present.

....

....

b) The test gives a cream precipitate.

i) Which halide ion is present? ....

ii) Write an ionic equation for the reaction. ....

Mixed Questions — Module C5

Q4 During a reaction, **0.12 g** of **magnesium** reacts completely with **20 cm³** of **nitric acid** to form **magnesium nitrate** and **hydrogen**. The acid is neutralised exactly.

$$Mg(s) + 2HNO_3(aq) \rightarrow Mg(NO_3)_2(aq) + H_2(g)$$

a) Calculate the number of moles of magnesium used.

....

b) Calculate the concentration of nitric acid used in **mol/dm³**.

....

c) **i)** Work out the relative formula mass of magnesium nitrate.

....

ii) Work out the mass of magnesium nitrate produced.

....

d) Calculate the volume of hydrogen gas formed (at RTP).

....

Q5 Brenda wants to find out the concentration of a solution of sodium hydroxide. She carries out a **titration** using **15 cm³** of **0.2 mol/dm³** hydrochloric acid, and finds that it takes **22 cm³** of sodium hydroxide to neutralise the acid.

a) Brenda started off with **2 mol/dm³** hydrochloric acid.
Describe how she could have made **100 cm³** of **0.2 mol/dm³** solution.

....

....

b) 1 mole of sodium hydroxide neutralises 1 mole of hydrochloric acid.
Calculate the concentration of the sodium hydroxide solution, in **mol/dm³**.

....

....

....

c) Calculate the concentration of the sodium hydroxide solution, in **g/dm³**.

....

....

Redox Reactions

Q1 Imagine that three new metals, **antium**, **bodium** and **candium** have been discovered. The relative **reactivity** of the three metals is shown on the right.

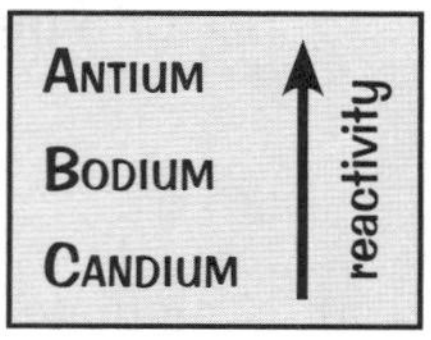

a) A piece of pure candium is put into a solution of bodium sulfate and left for 30 minutes. Circle the correct word in the pair to complete the sentence.

After the experiment, the solution contains **candium** / **bodium** sulfate.

b) If a piece of pure antium is put into a solution of candium sulfate, will any antium sulfate be formed? Explain your answer.

....

....

Q2 Join the terms in the centre to their correct descriptions. Some terms have more than one description.

removal of oxygen

addition of oxygen

a chemical that accepts electrons and becomes reduced

oxidation

reduction

oxidising agent

reducing agent

loss of electrons

a chemical that donates electrons and becomes oxidised

gain of electrons

Q3 A piece of **magnesium** is dropped into blue **copper(II) sulfate** ($CuSO_4$) solution.

Magnesium is <u>more reactive</u> than copper.

a) Write a **word equation** for the reaction that takes place.

....

b) Write a **balanced** symbol equation (including state symbols) for the reaction.

....

c) Are the magnesium atoms **oxidised** or **reduced** in this reaction?

....

Q4 Zinc reacts with iron(II) sulfate solution in a **redox reaction**. Iron is produced.

a) What is a '**redox reaction**'?

....

b) During this reaction, state which metal:

i) is oxidised. .... **ii)** gains electrons. ....

iii) is acting as an oxidising agent. ....

Redox Reactions

Q5 **Chlorine** reacts with **iron(II) ions** to produce **chloride ions** and **iron(III) ions**. This reaction can be represented by the equation: $Cl_2 + 2Fe^{2+} \rightarrow 2Cl^- + 2Fe^{3+}$.

During this reaction, state which element:

a) loses electrons.

....

b) is reduced.

....

c) is acting as a reducing agent.

....

Please Note:
Due to printing restriction, a "Red Ox" could not be shown on this page.
Please be amused by this grey goat instead.

Q6 Graham added equal amounts of **magnesium powder** into test tubes containing **metal chloride** solutions. His observations are shown in the table on the right.

Chloride solution	Observations
iron(II) chloride ($FeCl_2$)	Solution changes colour, and gets hotter. A precipitate forms.
calcium chloride ($CaCl_2$)	Nothing happens.

a) A reaction only took place when magnesium (Mg) was added to **iron(II) chloride solution**.

i) Write a **word equation** for the reaction that takes place.

....

ii) Write a **balanced** symbol equation (including state symbols) for the reaction.

....

b) When **magnesium** was added to **iron(II) chloride solution**, which metal was:

i) oxidised? ....

ii) reduced? ....

c) Using the information in the table, state whether calcium is **more** or **less reactive** than magnesium.

....

d) Copper is **less reactive** than magnesium, calcium and iron. Predict whether a reaction would take place if Graham added powdered **iron** to a solution of **copper chloride**.

....

Top Tips: OIL RIG: **O**xidation **I**s **L**oss of electrons, **R**eduction **I**s **G**ain of electrons. An absolutely blooming **vital** thing to remember. Otherwise you risk getting all mixed up on questions like these — and you don't want that, because there are bound to be questions like these in your exam.

Rusting of Iron

Q1 Paul carries out an experiment to investigate **rusting**. He puts three **iron** nails into separate test tubes, as shown in the diagram below.

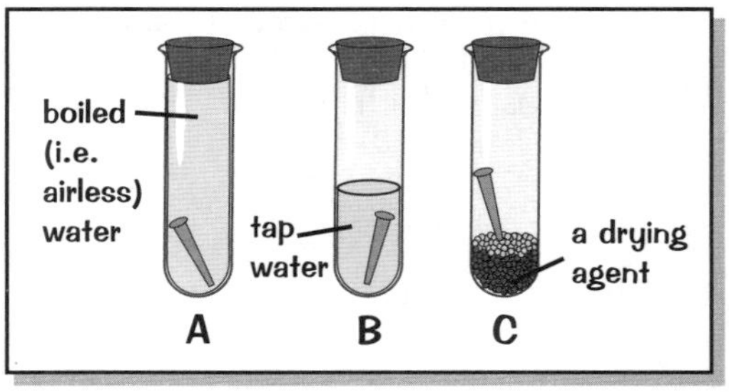

a) What **two** things are needed for iron to rust?

....

b) In which of these tubes will the iron rust most quickly?

....

c) Write a **word equation** for the formation of rust.

....

Q2 Tick the boxes to show whether each of the following statements is **true** or **false**.

	True	False
a) Painting metal items prevents them rusting by keeping out oxygen and water.	☐	☐
b) Rusting is a redox reaction.	☐	☐
c) Sacrificial protection involves a displacement reaction.	☐	☐
d) When iron rusts it loses two electrons to form Fe^{3+}.	☐	☐
e) When iron rusts the oxygen it reacts with is reduced and gains electrons.	☐	☐

Q3 Many different methods can be used to protect iron from rusting.

a) Explain why attaching magnesium bars to iron is known as 'the **sacrificial** method'.

....

b) Explain what galvanising is, and how it prevents iron from rusting.

....

....

c) Explain why coating iron with tin doesn't prevent rusting if the tin is scratched.

....

....

Q4 To prevent **iron** from rusting, it can be coated with **tin**, **paint** or **grease**. Alternatively, **magnesium bars** can be attached to the iron.

Explain which method would be most suitable for protecting **moving parts** on a very light glider.

....

....

Electrolysis

Q1 Circle the correct word(s) in each pair to complete the passage below.

During electrolysis of an ionic compound, an electric current is passed through a molten or **solid / dissolved** substance, causing it to **decompose / melt**. This **creates / prevents** a flow of charge through the **electrons / electrolyte**. Electrons are transferred to and from ions at the **electrodes / electrolytes**. As this happens atoms or **molecules / ions** are formed and **discharged / insulated** from the solution.

Q2 Tick the boxes to show whether these statements are **true** or **false**.

		True	False
a)	Positive ions move to the negative electrode and lose electrons.	☐	☐
b)	Negative ions move to the positive electrode and give up electrons.	☐	☐
c)	A salt will **only** conduct an electric current when molten.	☐	☐

Q3 **Sodium chloride solution** (brine) can electrolysed using the apparatus shown below.

a) Complete the labelling of the diagram.

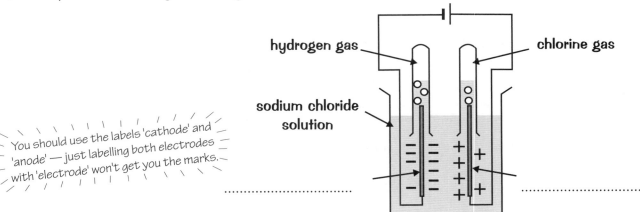

You should use the labels 'cathode' and 'anode' — just labelling both electrodes with 'electrode' won't get you the marks.

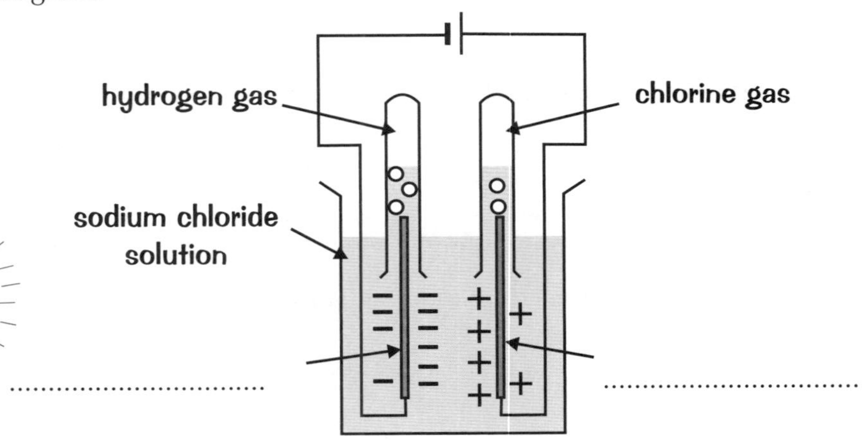

b) Complete the symbol equation for the reaction at the positive electrode:

.... Cl^- → Cl_2 + ... e^-

c) Sodium chloride can also be electrolysed when molten, but not when solid. Explain why this is.

....

....

Top Tips: More vital things to remember — the cathode is negative and gives up electrons, and the anode is positive and takes up electrons. Easy to remember if, like me, you don't like cats (the **cat**hode is **negative**). If you do like cats, then sorry — you'll have to think of another way.

Electrolysis

Q4 Complete the table to show the half equations at the cathode and anode during electrolysis of the following **molten** compounds.

Ions in molten substance	Product made at cathode	Half Equation	Product made at anode	Half-Equation
Na^+, Cl^-	sodium (Na)		chlorine (Cl_2)	
Pb^{2+}, Br^-	lead (Pb)		bromine (Br_2)	
Mg^{2+}, S^{2-}	magnesium (Mg)		sulfur (S)	
Al^{3+}, O^{2-}	aluminium (Al)		oxygen (O_2)	

Q5 Roy electrolyses aqueous **sulfuric acid**, H_2SO_4.

a) Give the formulas of the **three** ions present in this solution. ....

b) **i)** Which ion is discharged at the cathode? ....

ii) Write a balanced symbol equation for the reaction at the cathode.

....

c) **i)** Which ion is discharged at the anode? Explain your answer.

....

....

ii) Write a balanced symbol equation for the reaction at the anode.

....

Q6 Andrew is electrolysing a solution of **copper(II) sulfate** ($CuSO_4$). He uses two **carbon electrodes**.

a) Name all the substances that are being formed at:

i) the positive electrode. ....

ii) the negative electrode. ....

b) Write a balanced half-equation to show the reaction at:

i) the positive electrode: ....

ii) the negative electrode: ....

Electrolysis

Q7 The table below shows the **ions** present in **aqueous solutions** of sodium hydroxide. Use this table to answer the following questions on the **electrolysis** of sodium hydroxide.

Solution	Ions present
sodium hydroxide	Na^+, H^+, OH^-

a) State the gas formed at the anode. ....

b) Write a balanced half-equation for the reaction at the anode.

....

c) Where do the H^+ ions present in the solution come from? ....

d) Hydrogen is produced at the cathode. Explain why sodium is not produced at the cathode.

....

e) Write a balanced half-equation for the reaction at the cathode.

....

f) Circle the correct word in each pair to complete the following sentences.

i) Reduction takes place at the **anode** / **cathode**.

ii) Oxidation takes place at the **anode** / **cathode**.

Q8 **Electrolysis** breaks a compound down into new substances using **electricity**.

a) Give two ways you could increase the **amount** of a substance produced during electrolysis.

1. ....

2. ....

The formula for calculating the amount of charge transferred is:

$$\mathbf{Q = I \times t}$$

where **Q** is charge in coulombs (C), **I** is current in amps (A), and **t** is time in seconds (s).

b) Calculate the charge transferred when:

i) 2.5 A has flowed for 15 s. ....

ii) 0.1 A has flowed for 30 minutes. ....

c) Calculate the time (in minutes) 6 A needs to flow for to pass 4320 coulombs.

....

Electrolysis

Q9 **Copper(II) sulfate**, $CuSO_4$, was electrolysed to produce copper at the cathode. The table below shows the results of a set of experiments to determine how much copper was produced under different conditions.

Experiment number	Current (A)	Time (minutes)	Mass of cathode before experiment (g)	Mass of cathode after experiment (g)	Mass of copper produced (g)
1	0.4	40	5.14	5.46	
2	0.6	40	5.46	5.94	
3	0.8	40	5.94	6.58	
4	1.0	40	6.58	7.30	

a) i) Complete the table by calculating the mass of copper produced in each experiment.

ii) Use the table to draw a graph of the results.

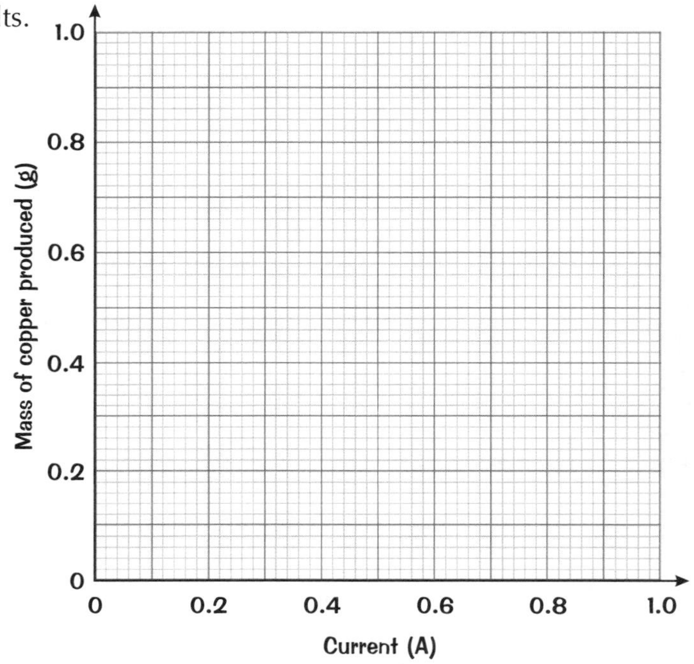

b) For one of the experiments, the current was set incorrectly.

i) Suggest which experiment was incorrect.

....

ii) Use your graph to find out the actual current used in the incorrect experiment.

....

Q10 **Silver nitrate** was electrolysed using a current of **0.8 amps**. A measuring cylinder was used to collect the oxygen that was given off from the anode.

After 50 minutes, 150 cm^3 of oxygen had been collected.

a) Calculate the volume of oxygen that would be collected after 80 minutes.

....

b) How many moles of oxygen is this?

1 mole of gas = 24 dm^3

....

Fuel Cells

Q1 **Energy level diagrams** can be used to represent different types of reaction.

a) Hydrogen and oxygen react together to produce water in an exothermic reaction. Sketch an energy level diagram to show this reaction.

b) The energy level diagram on the right shows the energy change when oxygen reacts with nitrogen to produce nitrogen monoxide. Is this reaction endothermic or exothermic? Explain your answer.

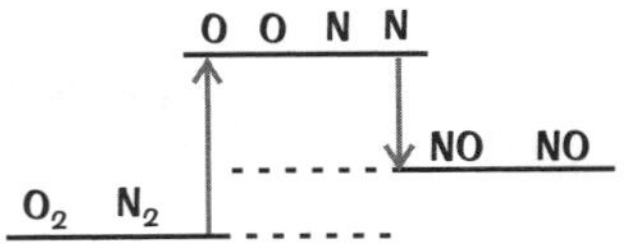

....

....

Q2 The diagram shows a hydrogen-oxygen **fuel cell**.

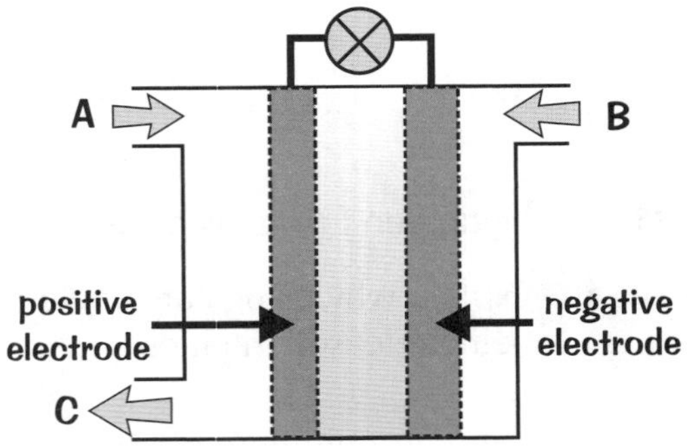

a) What goes into the cell at A and B?

A .... **B** ....

b) What comes out of the cell at C?

....

c) Complete the following sentence:

A hydrogen-oxygen fuel cell uses energy from the .... between hydrogen and oxygen to generate .... energy efficiently.

d) Write the word equation for the overall reaction that happens in the fuel cell.

....

e) Use the ions and molecules in the box on the right to write balanced symbol equations for the reactions at the:

O_2 OH^- e^- H_2O H_2

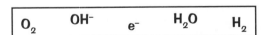

i) negative electrode. ....

ii) positive electrode. ....

f) Write a balanced symbol equation for the overall reaction that happens in the fuel cell.

....

g) Circle the correct words to complete the following sentence about the **electrodes** in a fuel cell.

Oxidation takes place at the **anode** / **cathode**, and reduction takes place at the **anode** / **cathode**.

Fuel Cells

Q3 Draw lines to connect the two halves of these sentences about **hydrogen-oxygen fuel cells**.

Fuel cells are more efficient than...

In a fuel cell electricity is generated...

Fuel cells waste less heat energy...

Fuel cells have no moving parts...

Fuel cells produce only water...

...so there is no harmful pollution.

...batteries or power stations.

...so no energy is lost due to friction.

...directly from the reaction.

...as they use fewer stages.

Q4 Give three advantages of using hydrogen fuel cells on **spacecraft**.

1. ....

2. ....

3. ....

Q5 Hydrogen fuel cells have some **environmental benefits** and some **environmental disadvantages**.

a) Explain why using cars powered by hydrogen fuel cells could lead to **less** carbon dioxide being released in cities.

....

....

b) Suggest a reason why using cars powered by hydrogen fuel cells might **not** actually **reduce** carbon dioxide emissions.

....

....

....

c) Describe **one** other possible environmental problem with hydrogen fuel cells.

....

....

d) Fossil fuels are a non-renewable energy source.
Give one reason why we will not run out of hydrogen for fuel cells.

....

....

CFCs and the Ozone Layer

Q1 **CFCs** are a **useful** group of chemicals.

a) Which of the following shows the formula of a CFC? Circle your answer.

CH_3Cl CH_3F CCl_2F_2 CH_2Cl_2

b) Which of the following are useful properties of CFCs? Circle your answer.

chemically inert | soluble in water | high boiling point

c) Give **two** uses of CFCs.

....

Q2 Say whether the following statements about **ozone** are **true** or **false**.

	True	False
a) Ozone is a form of oxygen with the formula O_3.	☐	☐
b) Most ozone is found in the lower part of the Earth's atmosphere.	☐	☐
c) Ozone does the important job of absorbing infrared light from the Sun.	☐	☐
d) When ozone absorbs the Sun's energy it breaks up into an oxygen molecule and an oxygen atom.	☐	☐

Q3 The thinning of the ozone layer is **dangerous**.

a) How does the thinning of the ozone layer affect the amount of UV radiation reaching the Earth?

....

b) Give two medical problems associated with this problem.

1. ....

2. ....

Q4 Choose from the words in the box to fill in the gaps in the passage below.

stratosphere	ions	infrared	thousands	unreactive
reactive	free radicals	one	troposphere	ultraviolet

CFCs are .... However, in the .... where there is lots of high-energy .... light, they break up to form .... Each CFC molecule produces one or more chlorine atoms which can react with .... of ozone molecules.

CFCs and the Ozone Layer

Q5 **Replacements** for CFCs are being developed.

a) Circle **two** substances from the list below that are thought to be suitable replacements for CFCs.

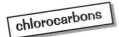

chlorocarbons | alkanes | trichlorides | alkenes | hydrofluorocarbons

b) One of the substances in the above list is a group of compounds that are very similar to CFCs. What is the important difference that makes these compounds safe to use?

....

Q6 **Free radicals** are very reactive particles.

a) Which of the dot-and-cross diagrams below correctly shows the formation of a chlorine free radical?

....

Diagram 1

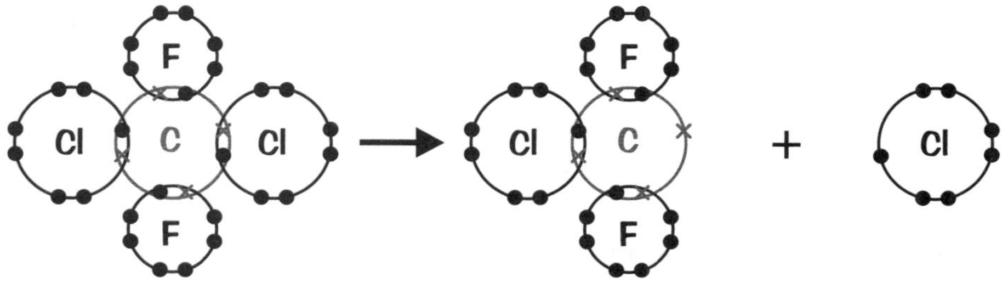

Diagram 2

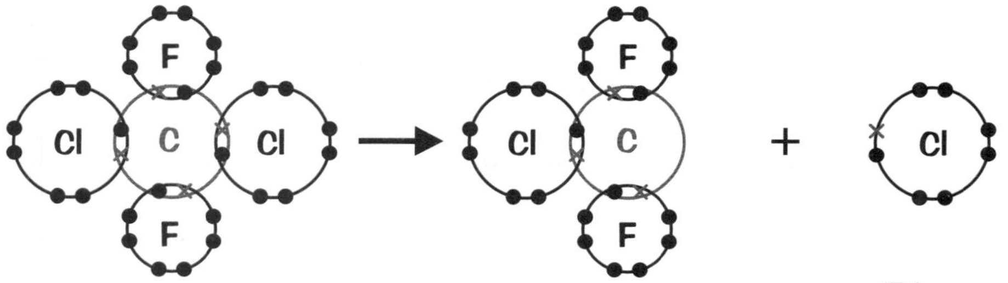

(Diagrams show outer electrons only)

b) Use the following terms to **label Diagram 1** and **2**.

Carbon-chlorine bond | **Highly reactive chlorine atom** | **Chlorine ion** | **Unpaired electron**

c) Write an equation to show what happens to CCl_2F_2 when UV light hits it.

....

d) Circle the correct word to complete the following sentence:

A chlorine radical is a chlorine **ion** / **atom** / **molecule** / **compound**.

CFCs and the Ozone Layer

Q7 CFCs damage the **ozone layer**.

a) Describe why scientists originally thought CFCs were safe to use.

....

....

....

b) Explain why even a complete ban on CFCs will not stop the damage to the ozone layer.

....

....

Q8 Circle the correct word(s) from each pair below to complete the statements about how scientists' attitudes to CFCs have **changed**.

a) In the 1970s scientists discovered that **carbon** / **chlorine** atoms can help to destroy ozone.

b) In the mid 1980s evidence was found which suggested that levels of ozone over Antarctica were **increasing** / **decreasing**.

c) Measurements in the upper atmosphere showed **high** / **low** levels of compounds produced by the breakdown of CFCs. This convinced scientists that CFCs **were** / **were not** linked to ozone depletion.

d) World leaders slowly **accepted** / **rejected** this evidence and began to ban the use of **CFCs** / **HFCs**.

Q9 **Free radicals** found in the upper atmosphere are responsible for the depletion of the ozone layer.

a) Briefly describe what's happening in the reactions below:

i) $O_3 + Cl\cdot \rightarrow ClO\cdot + O_2$

....

ii) $ClO\cdot + O_3 \rightarrow 2O_2 + Cl\cdot$

....

b) Explain why a few chlorine radicals can destroy a lot of ozone molecules.

....

....

Top Tips: CFCs were ideal for many uses — but we didn't fully understand what wider effects they'd have. Now there are loads of CFCs in the upper atmosphere, and we can't do much about it.

Hardness of Water

Q1 Tick the correct boxes to show whether the statements are **true** or **false**.

		True	False
a)	Rainwater which passes over limestone and chalk rocks becomes hard.	☐	☐
b)	Water can be softened by removing chloride and carbonate ions from the water.	☐	☐
c)	Adding sodium chloride is one way of removing hardness from water.	☐	☐
d)	Limescale is formed when soap is used with hard water.	☐	☐
e)	You can remove the hardness from water by adding sodium carbonate.	☐	☐

Q2 An **ion exchange column** can be used to remove the hardness from water.

a) Explain how hard water becomes soft when it is passed through an **ion exchange column**.

....

....

b) Does this method work for permanent hardness, temporary hardness, or both?

....

Q3 **Minerals** dissolve in water as it flows over rocks and through soil.

a) Give the **word equation** for the formation of soluble calcium hydrogencarbonate in this water.

....

b) Name the type of hardness that is caused by dissolved calcium hydrogencarbonate.

....

c) Name the type of hardness that is caused by dissolved calcium sulfate.

....

d) Washing soda is sometimes added to hard water.

i) Give the **chemical name** of washing soda.

....

ii) Describe the effect that washing soda has on hard water.

....

....

Top Tips: Hard water isn't very exciting, but at least it's not, well, hard. The only bits that will take some learning are the equations, especially that rather nasty calcium hydrogencarbonate one.

Hardness of Water

Q4 A teacher wanted to demonstrate how chalk (composed of $CaCO_3$) dissolves in rainwater to produce **hard water**, and how it forms **limescale** when it is boiled. She carried out the following experiments.

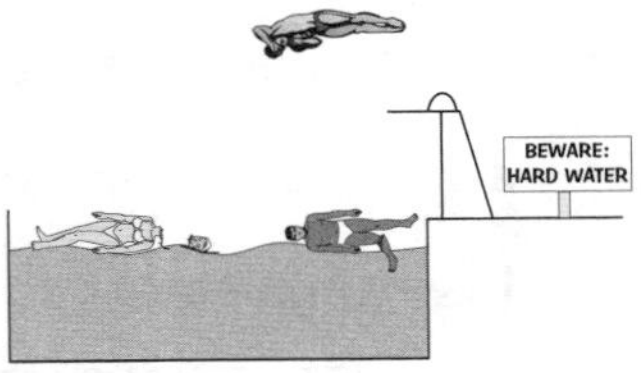

a) A spatula measure of powdered calcium carbonate was added to some distilled water and stirred. Explain why the water didn't become hard.

....

b) Carbon dioxide was bubbled through the mixture of calcium carbonate and distilled water. Explain why the water became hard.

....

....

c) A solution of calcium hydrogencarbonate was boiled in a beaker. The water became soft and a white precipitate formed.

i) Give the balanced symbol equation for this reaction. Include state symbols.

....

ii) Explain why the water became soft.

....

Q5 In an experiment to investigate the **hardness** of water from different sources, soap solution was added to samples of water. Five drops were added at a time until a good lather was formed when the samples were shaken. The experiment was then repeated with new samples of the water that had first been boiled.

Source of fresh water sample	Drops of soap solution needed to produce a lather
distilled water	5
Spondovia	35
Bogglewash	30
Oakbrook	5

Source of boiled water sample	Drops of soap solution needed to produce a lather
distilled water	5
Spondovia	35
Bogglewash	5
Oakbrook	5

a) What role did the test using distilled water play in the experiment?

....

b) **i)** Which source or sources contained **hard** water? ....

ii) Explain your answer to part **i)**.

....

c) **i)** Which source or sources contained **permanently hard** water? ....

ii) Explain your answer to part **ii)**.

....

Alcohols

Q1 **Alcohols** are a common group of chemicals.

a) Write out the general formula of an alcohol. ....

b) Complete the following table. Ethanol has been done for you.

Alcohol	No. of Carbon Atoms	Molecular Formula	Displayed Formula
Methanol	1		
Ethanol	2	C_2H_5OH	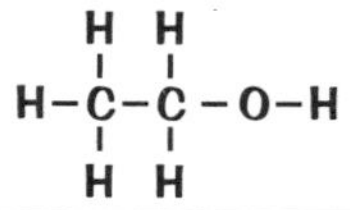
Propanol	3		
Butanol	4		
Pentanol	5		

Q2 The molecular formula for **ethanol** can be written as **C_2H_5OH** or as **C_2H_6O**.

a) What is the functional group found in all alcohols? ....

b) Explain why it is better to write ethanol's formula as C_2H_5OH.

....

Q3 Ethanol can be made industrially by **hydrating ethene** (C_2H_4).

a) Write the **word equation** for the hydration of ethene.

....

b) Write a **balanced symbol equation** for the hydration of ethene.

....

c) Briefly describe how the reaction is carried out.

....

....

Top Tips: You may be surprised to hear that the main use of ethanol is as a **motor fuel** and **fuel additive** — not in alcoholic drinks as I previously thought. It's also used as a solvent and antiseptic.

Alcohols

Q4 Choose from the words in the box to fill in the gaps in the passage below about **fermentation**.

inactive	25 °C	35 °C	50 °C	temperature	distilled
oxygen	hot	cold	glucose solution	enzymes	ethanoic acid

Fermentation is used to turn .... into ethanol. The reaction is catalysed by .... found in yeast cells. The .... needs to be carefully controlled during the reaction — if it is too .... the yeast are .... and the reaction is very slow, but if it is too .... the yeast enzymes are denatured. The optimum is between .... and .... It is important to stop .... getting into the reaction mixture, because it converts the ethanol to .... (CH_3COOH). The reaction stops when the concentration of the ethanol gets high enough to kill the yeast cells. Then the mixture can be .... to get pure ethanol.

Q5 **Ethanol** is produced on an industrial scale to make **alcoholic drinks** and **fuel for cars**.

a) The ethanol in alcoholic drinks is produced by **fermenting glucose**.

i) Write a word equation for this reaction.

....

ii) Write a balanced symbol equation for this reaction.

....

b) The ethanol used in car fuels can be made by **fermenting glucose** or by **hydrating ethene**.

i) Which method of producing ethanol is more **sustainable**? Explain your answer.

....

....

ii) Which method has the best **atom economy**? Explain your answer.

....

....

iii) Fermentation is a **batch** production process and ethene hydration a **continuous** production process. Briefly explain the advantages and disadvantages of each process.

....

....

....

Fats and Oils

Q1 Fats and oils come from **plants** and **animals**.

a) Name one fat or oil that comes from plants and one that comes from animals.

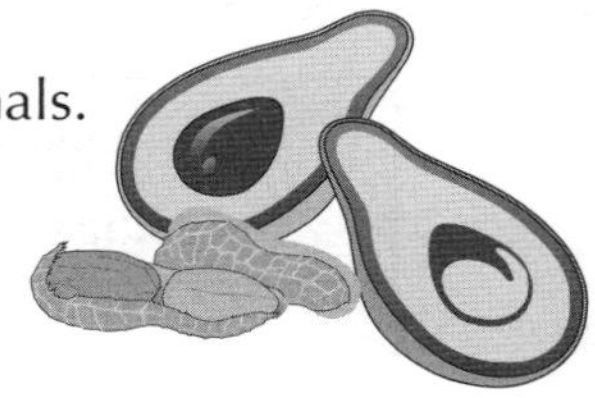

Plants: ....

Animals: ....

b) Give two uses of natural fats and oils.

1. ....

2. ....

Q2 Complete the passage below using some of the words in the box.

alcohols	fatty	strong	solids	acids	glycerol
esters	liquids	ethanol	gases	alkenes	

Fats are .... at room temperature and oils are ....
Fats and oils are members of a group of chemicals called ....
These chemicals can be made by reacting together .... and
.... Hydrolysis breaks up fats and oils into ....
acids and ....

Q3 Butter and milk are **emulsions** of oil and water.

a) Oil and water are **immiscible** — what does this mean?

....

b) Describe what an emulsion is, and how to make one.

....

....

c) Look at the diagrams below. Label the droplets of **oil** and the droplets of **water**.

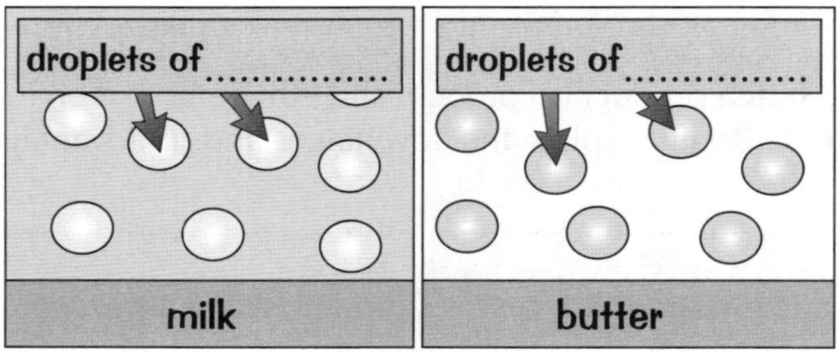

Fats and Oils

Q4 Vegetable oils can be turned into **fuels**.

a) Name **one** fuel that can be made from vegetable oils.

....

b) Name a fossil fuel that your answer to part **a)** can be used as an alternative for.

....

c) A litre of "**Supreme**" biofuel contains **70%** of the energy that is found in a litre of the fossil fuel "**Megamax**". "**Megamax**" contains 37 MJ (37 000 000 J) of energy per litre. Calculate how much energy a litre of "**Supreme**" biofuel contains.

....

Q5 Oils and fats can be used to make **soap**.

a) What is **saponification**?

....

....

b) Draw lines to connect the two parts of the following sentences.

Soap is made by...	...boiling oil or fat with alkali.
The alkali usually used is...	...glycerol is produced.
As well as soap...	...sodium hydroxide.

c) Write the word equation for making soap.

....

d) Circle the correct word(s) from each pair to complete the sentences about **making soap**.

Fat molecules can be broken apart to give glycerol and fatty acids — this is an example of a **neutralisation** / **hydrolysis** reaction. The **glycerol** / **fatty acids** can then react with **sodium hydroxide** / **hydrochloric acid** to form soap.

Top Tips: Fats are horrible. Like when you get a nice shoulder of lamb, but you can't eat half of it because it's all fat. And then you go and learn that when you're using soap, you're kind of washing your hands with fat. Ugghh. On second thoughts, I don't think anything could beat some butter spread thickly over some freshly baked bread... ummm...

Using Plant Oils

Q1 Circle the correct word in each pair below to label each fatty acid structure.

a) **Saturated / unsaturated** grape seed oil

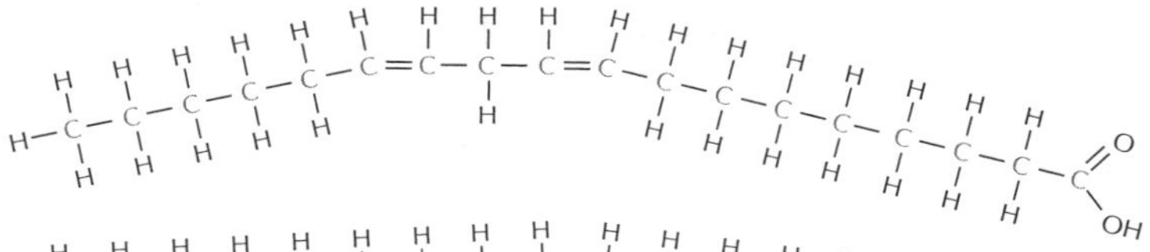

b) **Saturated / unsaturated** olive oil

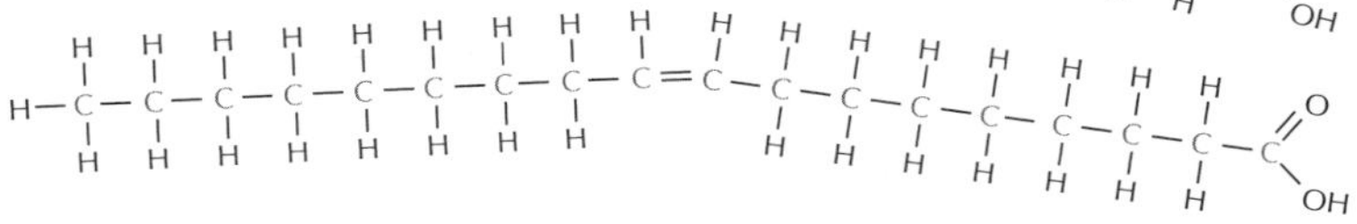

c) **Saturated / unsaturated** animal fat

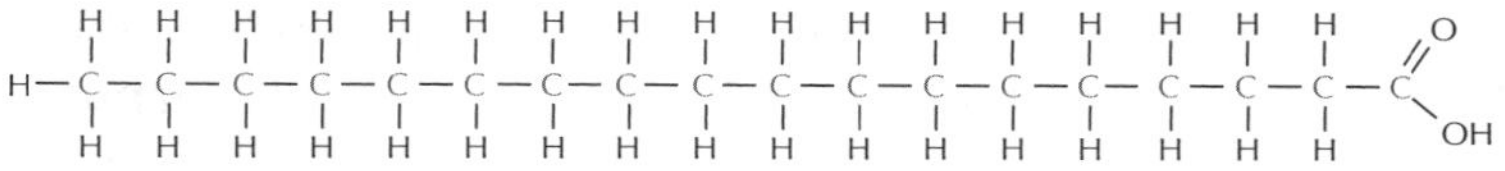

Q2 Ben has two test tubes. One contains a sample of an **unsaturated fat** and the other has a sample of a **saturated fat**. He adds some **bromine water** to both tubes and shakes them.

a) After Ben added the bromine water, the substance in the **first test tube** stayed orange. State whether the substance in the **first tube** is a sample of saturated fat or unsaturated fat.

b) **i)** Describe what you would see happening in the **second test tube** as Ben shakes it.

ii) Briefly describe the reaction that is taking place in the **second test tube**.

Q3 Margarine is usually made from **partially hydrogenated** vegetable oil.

a) Describe how hydrogenation is carried out.

b) Describe how hydrogenation affects the chemical structure of vegetable oils.

Q4 State which are less healthy, **saturated** or **unsaturated** fats. Explain your answer.

Detergents

Q1 Tick the boxes to show whether these statements about **dry cleaning** are **true** or **false**.

	True	False
a) **Dry cleaning** means any cleaning process that involves using **water** as a **solvent**.	☐	☐
b) **Dry cleaning** can be used to remove **stains** that will not **dissolve** in **water**.	☐	☐
c) There are **strong intermolecular forces** between the molecules in a **grease** stain.	☐	☐
d) Molecules **of dry cleaning solvents** have **weak intermolecular forces** between them.	☐	☐
e) As you add the solvent, **intermolecular forces** form between the solvent molecules and the grease molecules.	☐	☐
f) When the **solvent** is removed the **grease molecules** are left behind.	☐	☐

Q2 The diagram shows a **detergent molecule**.

a) Complete the diagram by labelling the **hydrophilic** and **hydrophobic** sections of the molecule.

....  ....

b) Explain how the structure of a detergent molecule helps it to remove oily stains in the wash.

....

....

....

Q3 Felicity works for a chemical company that is developing a new **washing powder**. She tests five different powders and records their **cleaning effectiveness** at different temperatures against a range of stains. She uses a scale of **1** (**poor**) to **10** (**excellent**).

a) Felicity's results are shown in the table on the right.

i) State which powder is best at cleaning grass stains at 30 °C.

....

ii) Which powders contain **enzymes**? Explain your answer.

....

....

....

		Washing powder				
		A	**B**	**C**	**D**	**E**
Effectiveness	**Stain: tomato Temperature: 30 °C**	8	3	5	8	8
	Stain: tomato Temperature: 50 °C	3	3	9	8	3
	Stain: grass Temperature: 30 °C	7	4	5	8	9
	Stain: grass Temperature: 50 °C	3	4	8	9	3

b) Some of the washing powders work best at lower temperatures. Give two advantages of being able to wash your clothes at lower temperatures.

1. ....

2. ....

Mixed Questions — Module C6

Q1 Sam is using **electrolysis** to split **lead(II) iodide** (PbI_2) into **pure solid lead** and **iodine gas**.

a) Sam has to melt the lead(II) iodide before he can electrolyse it.
Explain why he cannot electrolyse **solid** lead(II) iodide.

....

....

b) Sam's molten lead(II) iodide contains **lead ions** (**Pb^{2+}**) and **iodide ions** (**I^-**).

i) State whether the solid lead is formed at the **anode** or at the **cathode**. ....

ii) Write the half-equation for the reaction that takes place at the **anode**.

....

c) Lead is **more reactive** than copper. Describe what will happen to the metals if Sam adds some of his pure lead to a solution of copper chloride.

....

....

Q2 **Hydrogen-oxygen fuel cells** involve a **redox reaction**.

a) Draw a line to join each electrode to the correct half-equation for the reaction that takes place there.

$O_2 + 2H_2 \rightarrow 2H_2O$ | **Cathode** | $O_2 + 4e^- + 2H_2O \rightarrow 4OH^-$

$2H_2 + 4OH^- \rightarrow 4H_2O + 4e^-$ | **Anode** | $2H_2O \rightarrow O_2 + 2H_2$

b) Explain why the reaction is classed as a **redox reaction**.

....

....

c) Give one **advantage** of using hydrogen fuel cells instead of petrol to power a car engine.

....

Q3 The Forth Rail Bridge is the second longest cantilever bridge in the world. It is made of over 50 000 tonnes of **steel**, it is 2.5 km long and it is **painted** all over.

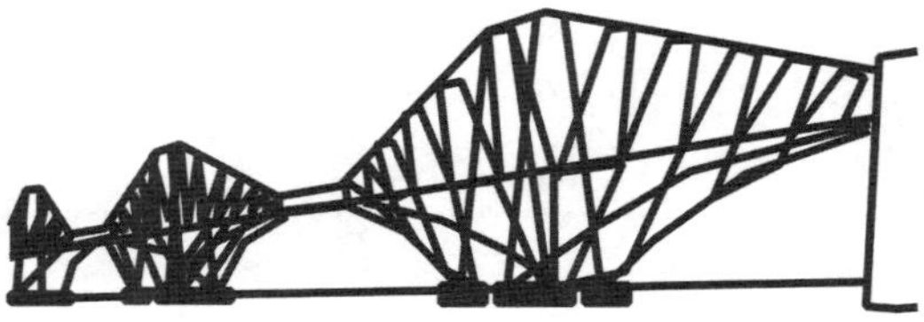

a) Give one reason why it is necessary to paint the bridge.

....

b) Another type of steel is used for making cutlery, but this doesn't need to be painted. Explain why.

....

....

Mixed Questions — Module C6

Q4 The diagram opposite shows the electrolysis of **copper(II) sulfate solution**, with copper electrodes.

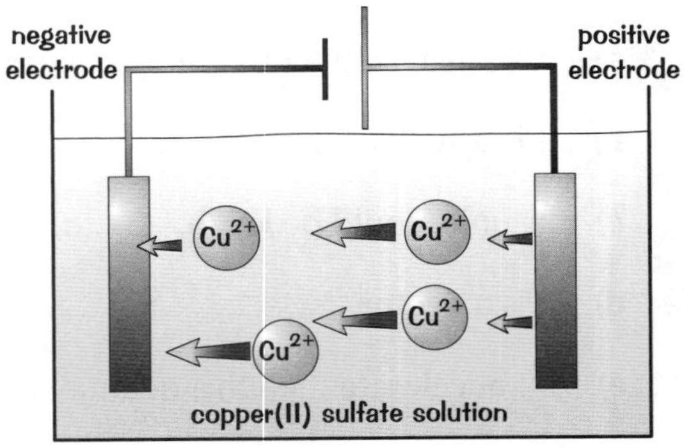

a) Complete the half-equations for the reaction at each electrode.

i) At the positive electrode:

Cu → .... + ...

ii) At the negative electrode:

Cu^{2+} + ... → ....

b) i) If 5 g of copper formed at the negative electrode, state the mass of copper that was lost from the positive electrode.

....

ii) If 2 amps flows through the solution of copper(II) sulfate for 30 minutes, 1.2 g of copper is formed at the negative electrode. Calculate how long it would take for **5 g** of copper to form if a current of **5 amps** flows through the solution.

....

....

....

....

Q5 **Chlorine free radicals** act on ozone in the stratosphere.

a) Briefly describe how chlorine free radicals are produced from CFCs.

....

b) One chlorine free radical can break up a large number of ozone molecules. Why is this?

....

....

c) Since the 1990s, butane has been used as a propellant in aerosols in Europe.

i) Explain why alkanes are a better alternative to CFCs.

....

ii) Suggest another safe alternative to CFCs.

....

Speed and Velocity

Q1 Write down whether each of the following statements applies to **speed** only, **velocity** only or **both**.

a) It changes if the **direction** changes. ....

b) It is a **scalar**. ....

c) Its units could be **km/h**. ....

d) It is a **vector**. ....

e) If I **accelerate** then this quantity **must** change. ....

f) If I **accelerate** this quantity **might not** change. ....

Q2 Describe the difference between a **scalar** and a **vector** quantity.

....

....

Q3 The **speed–time** graph below shows two cars (A and B) **accelerating** away from traffic lights.

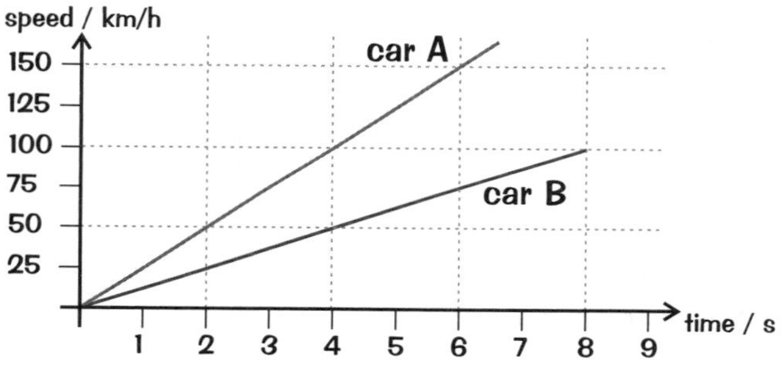

a) How **fast** was car A going at **4 s**?

....

b) How fast was car B going at this time?

....

c) If the cars were going in the **same direction**, what would be car A's speed relative to car B **at 4 s**?

....

....

d) If the cars were going in **opposite** directions, what would their relative speed be at **6 seconds**?

....

....

Combining Velocities and Forces

Q1 Work out the **size** and **direction** of the resultant force acting on the pots of jam shown below.

a)

Size of force .... N

Direction: ....

b)

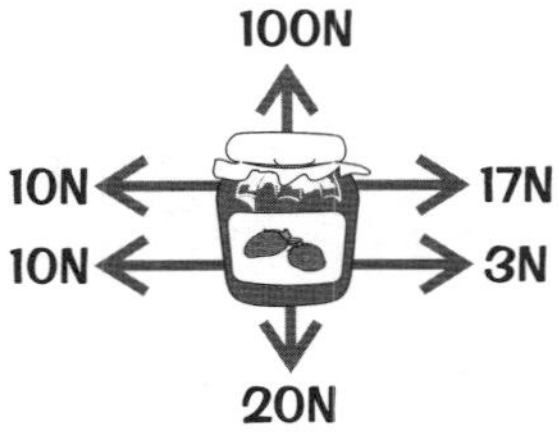

Size of force .... N

Direction: ....

Q2 Greta swims at **1 m/s** to the **East** along a river. Ray stands on the riverbank and watches her.

a) How **fast** is Greta swimming relative to Ray if the river is flowing at **1.5 m/s** due **East**?

Velocity = ... m/s Direction = ...

b) How fast is Greta swimming relative to Ray if the river is flowing **2.0 m/s** due **West**?

Velocity = ... m/s Direction = ...

Q3 **Forces** and **velocities** can be combined in **vector** diagrams.

a) A glider is flying at **10 m/s** due **North** when it experiences a cross wind of **15 m/s** due **East**. Complete the vector diagram and use it to work out the **resultant velocity** of the glider — its **speed** and its new **bearing** (angle clockwise from North). Give your answers to the nearest whole number.

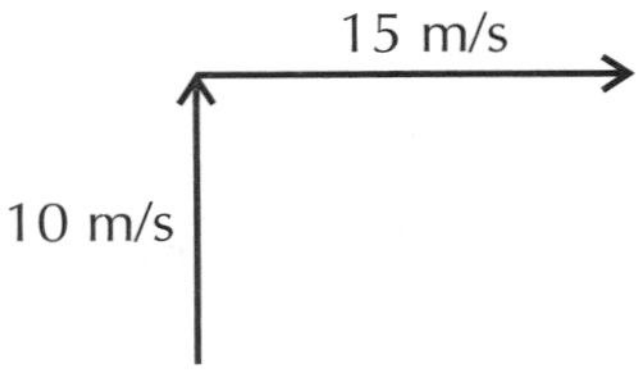

....

....

....

Resultant velocity = ... m/s on a bearing of ....°.

b) Emma swims across a river which is flowing **westwards** at **5 m/s**. She swims at **2 m/s**, heading directly across the river from point X.

Calculate Emma's resultant velocity — her **speed** and the **angle** between her direction of travel and the river bank. Give your answers to the nearest m/s and the nearest degree.

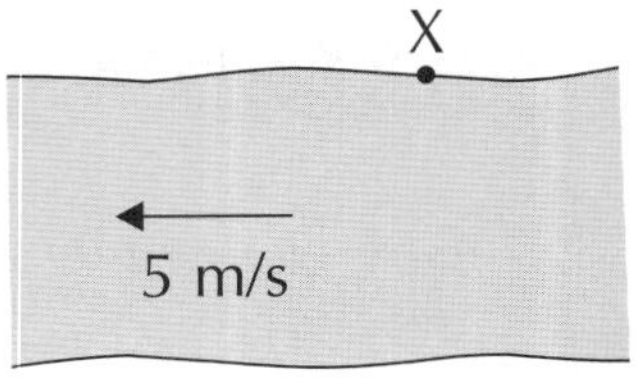

....

....

....

....

Equations of Motion

Q1 a) What **quantities** do the following **symbols** stand for in the equations of motion?

i) **s** stands for ....

ii) **u** stands for ....

iii) **v** stands for ....

iv) **t** stands for ....

v) **a** stands for ....

You should always stand for the national anthem.

b) Complete the four equations below.

s = ut +

s = ———— t

v = +

v^2 =

Q2 Choose the appropriate **equation** and **solve** the following.

You'll need to rearrange the equation for some of these.

a) Find s if u = 0 m/s, a = 5 m/s² and t = 20 s.

....

....

b) Find v if u = 20 m/s, a = 1 m/s² and s = 250 m.

....

....

c) Find t if s = 45 m, u = 3 m/s and v = 15 m/s.

....

....

d) Find a if s = 100 m, u = 0 m/s and t = 5 s.

....

....

Q3 A car accelerates at **2.5 m/s²** from rest. What speed will it have reached after **20 seconds**?

....

....

Q4 I throw a **banana** vertically up into the air at an initial speed of **10 m/s**.
It accelerates downwards at **10 m/s²**. Calculate the **maximum height** of the banana.

....

....

Projectile Motion

Q1 Choose from the words below to complete the passage.

friction	gravity	ground track	parabola	trajectory	hyperbola

The only **force** acting on a projectile is .... (ignoring air resistance).

The **path** a projectile follows is called its ....

The **shape** of this path is a ....

Q2 For each of these statements, tick **true** or **false** as appropriate.

		True	False
a)	Horizontal and vertical motion are totally separate — one doesn't affect the other.	☐	☐
b)	A bullet fired horizontally at 200 m/s will accelerate down to the ground at the same rate as a stone thrown horizontally at 1 m/s. (Ignore air resistance.)	☐	☐
c)	If something is thrown horizontally at 10 m/s, its initial vertical velocity is 10 m/s.	☐	☐
d)	The horizontal velocity remains constant for a projectile (ignoring air resistance).	☐	☐
e)	On Earth, an object will accelerate vertically towards the ground at about 10 m/s^2.	☐	☐

Q3 This diagram shows a regular pulse of water droplets that have been **projected** through the air.

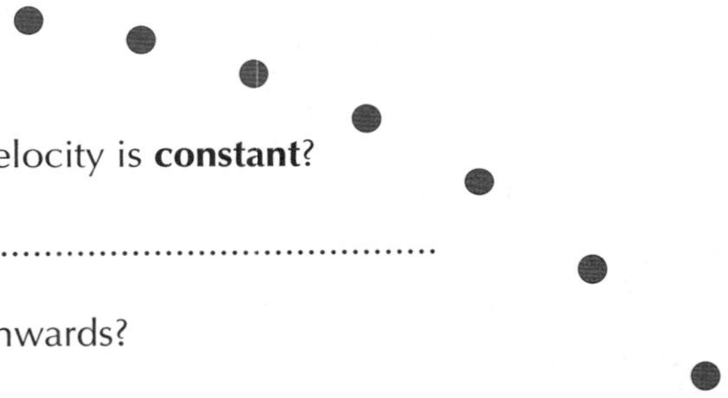

a) How can you tell from the diagram that the horizontal velocity is **constant**?

....

b) How can you tell that the droplets are **accelerating** downwards?

....

Q4 Which of the following are examples of **projectile motion**? Circle any which are.

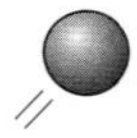

a football kicked towards the goal 

an orange rolling off a table

a cannonball fired from a cannon 

a powered plane flying over the Himalayas 

a football dribbled towards the goal 

a high jumper in flight 

Q5 A plane is carrying some water to try and put out a forest fire.
The plane is flying **horizontally** at a **velocity** of **80 m/s** and it is **125 m** above the ground.

a) Taking the acceleration due to **gravity** to be **10 m/s^2**, how long will it take the water to reach the ground once it has left the plane (ignoring air resistance)?

....

....

b) At what **distance** before the forest fire must the water be released?

....

Forces and Newton's Third Law

Q1 Complete the following passage.

When an object exerts a .... on another object, it experiences a force in return. The two forces are called an .... pair. For example, if someone leans on a wall with a force of 150 N, the wall exerts a force of .... N in the opposite direction. In a collision, colliding objects exert '............................ and ....' forces on each other.

Q2 A **flamingo** is standing on one leg. The force, **A**, is the flamingo pushing down on the ground.

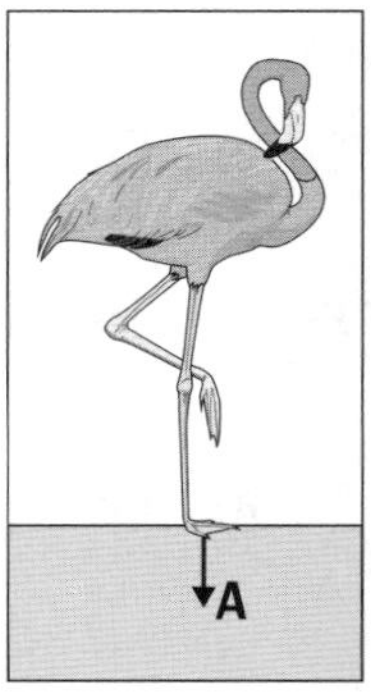

a) Add a labelled arrow B to show the other force in the interaction pair.

b) Complete the following sentences about the two forces:

Force A is exerted by the flamingo on the ....

Force B is exerted by the .... on the ....

Q3 Complete the following passage by circling the correct word(s) in each pair.

When a gun is fired, the bullet exerts a force on the gun that is **different** / **equal** and **opposite to** / **in the same direction as** the force exerted by the gun on the bullet. The bullet travels out of the barrel and the gun recoils in the **opposite** /**same** direction.

Q4 Burning fuel in a rocket engine produces **hot gases** which accelerate **downwards** from the engine.

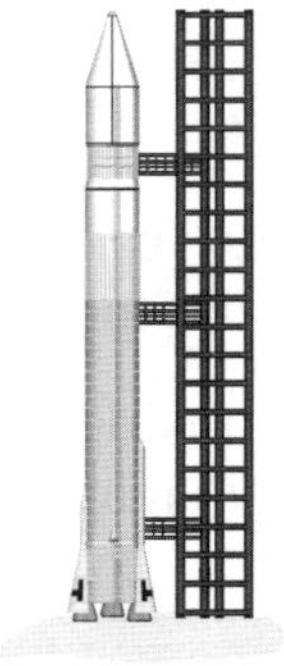

a) Complete this sentence by circling the correct word(s).

The hot gases get pushed downwards out of the exhaust because the **air** / **rocket engine wall** exerts **a force** / **friction** on them.

b) Explain how this process makes a rocket move **upwards**.

....

....

....

Conservation of Momentum

Q1 Claire (mass **55 kg**) is standing on a skateboard (mass **5 kg**) at rest. She then jumps forwards off the skateboard at **1.8 m/s**.

a) What was the **total momentum** of Claire and the skateboard before she jumped?

....

b) What was Claire's momentum **after** she jumped?

Momentum (kg m/s) = mass (kg) × velocity (m/s)

....

c) Calculate the **final** momentum of the skateboard.

....

Q2 A **90 g** apple is fired at **10 m/s** from a stationary toy cannon which has mass **2 kg**. The cannon recoils (moves **backwards**) as the apple is fired.

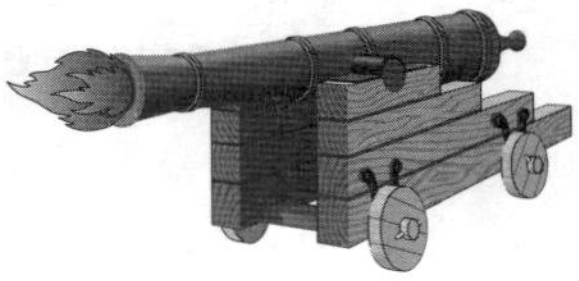

a) Explain why the cannon **recoils**.

....

....

b) Calculate how **fast** the cannon will move backwards.

....

....

Q3 A **900 kg** car travelling at **9 m/s** collides with a fence. The car is slowed down to **8.5 m/s** by the collision and the fence becomes **attached** to the car. Calculate the **mass** of the fence.

You can assume the fence was stationary before the collision.

....

....

....

Q4 Two roller skaters, Karl (**72 kg**) and Jenny (**48 kg**), are moving towards one another. Jenny is travelling at **4 m/s**. Karl runs into Jenny and they move together in the direction that Karl was travelling before the collision at **0.5 m/s**. Find how **fast** Karl was moving **before** the collision.

....

....

....

Top Tips: Momentum is like the barn owl — it's conserved, as long as no external forces act. Imagine a stationary owl — zero momentum. Now imagine a bulldozer acting on the owl and coalescing with it — the momentum of the owl and bulldozer together is conserved (but the owl isn't).

Pressure

Q1 Fill in the blanks with some of the words provided to complete the statements below.

Quantum	empty	Kinetic	collide	random	small	large	boring

.... theory says that gases consist of very .... particles.

These particles are constantly moving in completely .... directions.

They constantly .... with each other and with the walls of their container.

The particles hardly take up any room so most of the gas is .... space.

Q2 The apparatus shown in the diagram can be used to show how **pressure** changes with **temperature** for a gas.

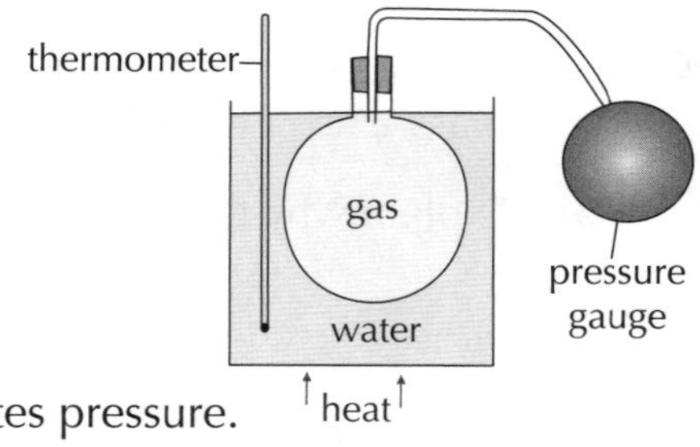

a) What variable is kept **constant** by having the gas in a rigid sealed container? Circle the correct letter.

A Pressure **B** Volume **C** Temperature

b) Explain how the **movement** of gas particles in the container creates pressure.

....

....

....

c) If the thermometer reading **increases**, what will happen to the **pressure** of the gas? Explain why.

....

....

....

d) State how the pressure of the gas would change if its **volume** was **decreased**, and explain why. Assume that the **temperature** is kept **constant**.

....

....

....

The pressure was getting to David and Freddie.

Q3 Explain how the **pressure** of a gas is related to the **change in momentum** of gas particles.

....

....

Gravity and Orbits

Q1 Indicate whether the following statements about gravity are **true** or **false**.

	True	False
a) Gravity can attract and repel other masses.	☐	☐
b) Gravity is a weak force and is only noticeable if one of the masses is really big.	☐	☐
c) Earth's gravity gets weaker the higher up you go.	☐	☐
d) All other things being equal, heavy things accelerate to the ground more quickly than lighter things.	☐	☐
e) The Sun's gravity makes the Earth orbit around it.	☐	☐
f) The Sun's gravity makes the Moon orbit the Earth.	☐	☐

Q2 This is a diagram of a planet **orbiting the Sun**.

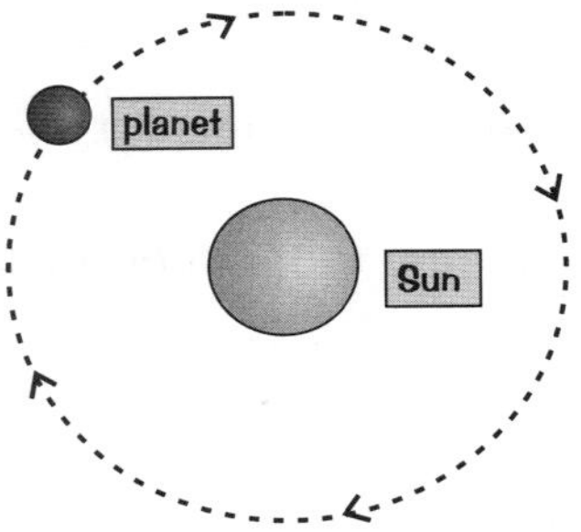

a) Draw an **arrow** on the diagram to show the direction of the Sun's **gravitational force** on the planet and label it 'F'.

b) Now draw an arrow showing the direction of the planet's **velocity** and label it 'V'.

c) i) What is the special name given to a force that makes an object move in a **circle**?

....

ii) In what **direction** does this force always act?

....

Q3 Here is a diagram of a comet's orbit around the Sun. **A**, **B**, **C** and **D** are different points on the orbit.

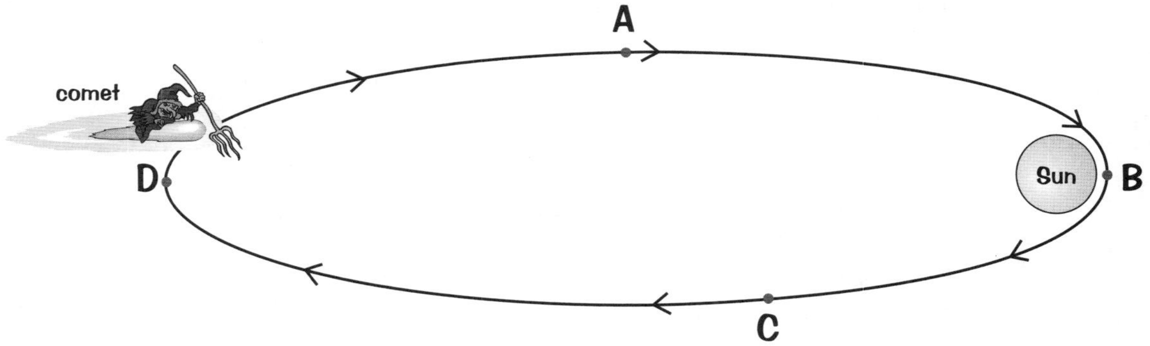

a) Answer each of the following questions with the correct letter A-D.

i) At which point on the orbit is the comet travelling the **slowest**? ....

ii) At which point on the orbit is the comet travelling the **quickest**? ....

b) Explain why the speed of the comet **changes** in different parts of its orbit.

....

....

Gravity and Orbits

Q4 The table below contains data about the **orbits** of **six** of the **planets** which orbit the Sun.

A.U. = astronomical unit — the distance from the Earth to the Sun.

	Mercury	Venus	Earth	Mars	Jupiter	Saturn
Distance from Sun (A.U)	0.39	0.72	1.00	1.52	5.20	9.54
Time for one orbit (Earth years)	0.24	0.62	1.00	1.88	11.9	29.5

What can you **conclude** from the **data**? Circle the letters of any of the following which apply.

A The further out the planet is from the Sun, the weaker the Sun's gravity.

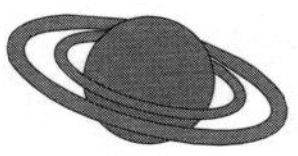

B The time it takes a planet to orbit the Sun is directly proportional to its distance from the Sun.

C The further out the planet is from the Sun, the longer it takes to orbit.

D Planets further out than Saturn will take longer than 29.5 years to orbit the Sun.

Be careful... The question is asking you what you can conclude from THIS data.

Q5 The force of gravity depends on the **distance** between masses.

a) If you **double** the distance you are from a planet, what happens to the **force** of its gravity on you?

b) A satellite **orbiting** the Earth feels a gravitational force of **250 N**. What gravitational force would the same satellite feel if its orbit were moved to be:

i) five times further away from the Earth?

ii) half the distance from the Earth?

Top Tips: This gravity stuff isn't as bad as it seems... Honest. Watch out with that old inverse square relationship though. Don't forget the "square" bit, or the "inverse" bit — it's easy to rush things and make a mistake and you wouldn't want to drop easy marks in the exam, would you.

Satellites

Q1 Some satellites have **geostationary** orbits. Others have **polar** orbits.

a) **i)** Complete the following by circling the correct words.

A geostationary satellite is in a **low** / **high** orbit over the Earth's **equator** / **poles**.

ii) Explain how polar-orbiting satellites can scan the **whole** of the Earth's surface every day.

....

....

....

b) On the diagram, draw the orbits of a **polar** satellite and a **geostationary** satellite.

Label the polar orbit '**P**' and the geostationary orbit '**G**'.

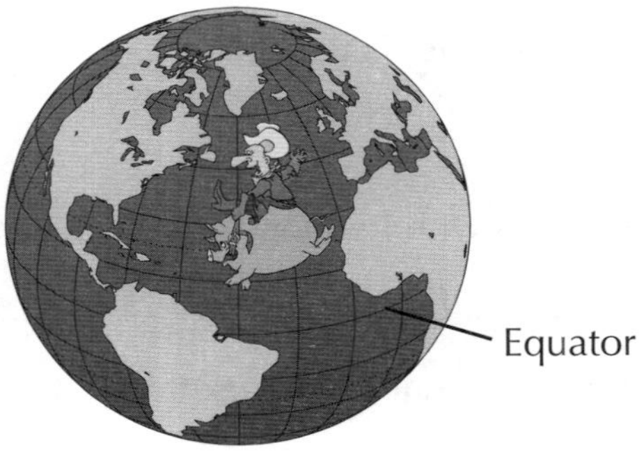

Q2 Answer the following questions on geostationary and polar orbits.

a) Why is it useful for a **communications** satellite to be in a geostationary orbit?

....

....

b) How long does a geostationary satellite take to make one **complete orbit** of the Earth?

....

c) Explain why the polar orbits of **spy satellites** need to be **low**.

....

....

Q3 **Satellites** are used to transmit signals between different places on the Earth.

a) What type of electromagnetic radiation is used to transmit satellite TV signals?

....

b) Explain how a satellite TV signal is transmitted from the main transmitter to a house on the other side of the country.

....

....

Radio Waves and Microwaves

Q1 **Electromagnetic** (EM) **waves**, such as **radio waves** and **microwaves**, are used to transmit different types of **communication signals**. Use the words below to fill in the blanks.

scattered **ionosphere** **radio** **reduces** **atmosphere** **30 GHz** **30 MHz** **line of sight** **absorbed** **curvature**

a) .... waves can reflect off a layer of the atmosphere called the .... This allows the wave to overcome the .... of the Earth. These waves have frequencies up to about ....

b) Electromagnetic waves with frequencies between 30 MHz and .... can pass easily through the .... This means transmissions must be by ....

c) Electromagnetic waves with frequencies above 30 GHz are .... and .... by rain and dust. This .... the strength of the signal, so the highest frequency that can be used for satellite transmissions is about 30 GHz.

Q2 One important property of waves is **diffraction**.

a) Circle the phrase that best describes what '**diffraction**' means.

The lowering of the amplitude of waves when passing through a gap.

The spreading out of waves when passing through a gap.

The converging of waves when they pass through a gap.

b) Describe the **conditions** required to achieve **maximum diffraction**.

....

....

c) A **ripple tank** is used to study the behaviour of waves as they pass through **gaps**. Both gaps are the **same size** as the **wavelength** of the wave coming towards them.

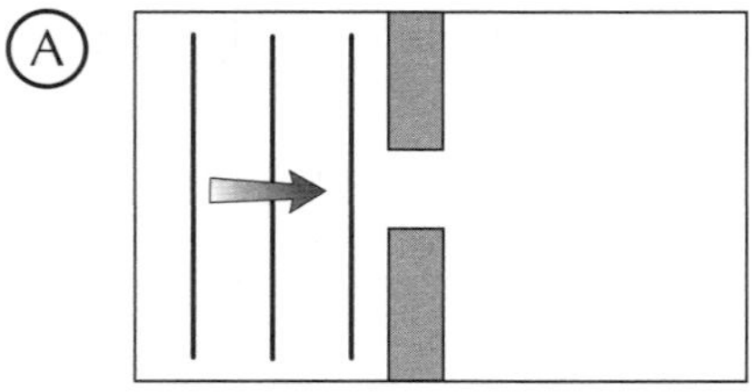

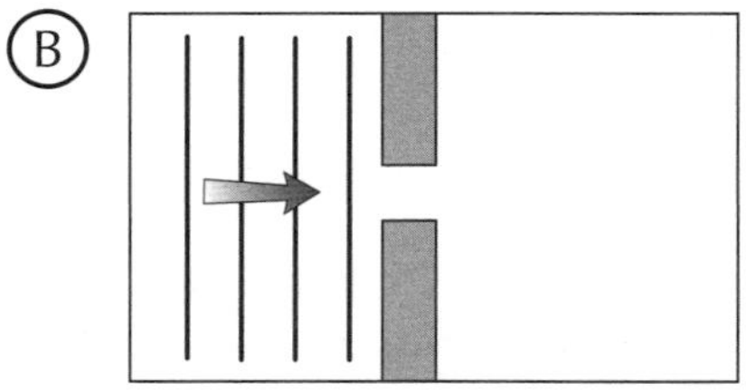

State which wave, **A** or **B**, will be diffracted the **most**. ....

Radio Waves and Microwaves

Q3 Satellite TV transmission uses **microwaves**.

a) Hardeep is getting satellite TV installed in his new house. He wants the satellite dish to go on the **back** of the house. The technician installing the dish explains that the dish must go on the **front** of the house, and must point at a **specific part of the sky**.

Explain why the satellite dish must face in a specific **direction**.

....

....

....

....

b) Explain why **frequencies above 30 GHz** can't be used to transmit signals from Earth to satellites.

....

....

....

Q4 **Long wave radio** has much **longer wavelengths** than **FM radio**.

a) Tick the boxes below to show which (if any) of the houses would receive long wave radio waves and which (if any) would receive FM radio waves.

	long wave	FM
House A	☐	☐
House B	☐	☐

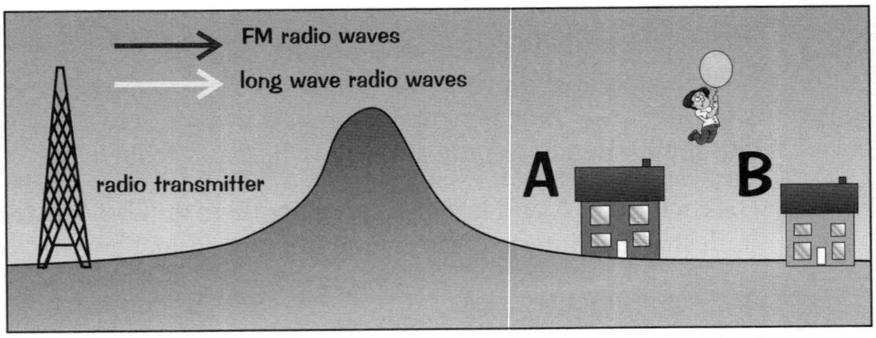

b) Explain why long wave radio has a longer range than FM radio.

....

....

....

Top Tips: Electromagnetic waves are pretty darn useful — they make TV, radio and mobile phones work. But you have to know which frequency waves can be used to do each job. Otherwise you'd end up with fuzzy satellite TV and then how would you watch Notts County thrash Man U...

Interference of Waves

Q1 The diagrams below each show **displacement–time** graphs of two waves that are **overlapping**.

On each set of empty axes, draw what the graph of the **combined** wave would look like.
Also decide whether the interference is **constructive** or **destructive** — circle the correct answer.

a)

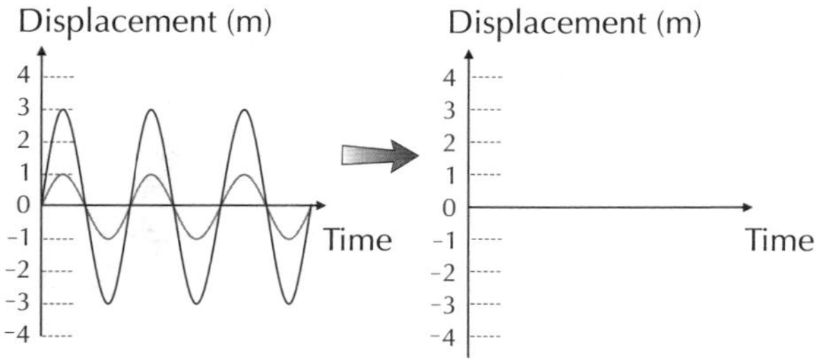

This is **constructive** / **destructive** interference.

b)

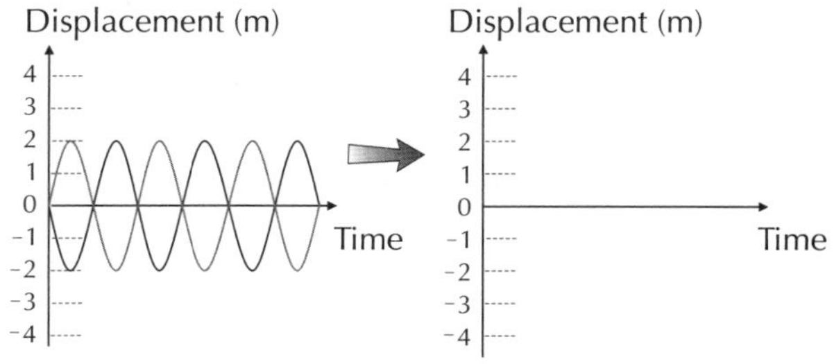

This is **constructive** / **destructive** interference.

Q2 Tick the boxes to show whether the following sentences are **true** or **false**.

	True	False
a) Monochromatic light can't be used to show stable interference patterns.	☐	☐
b) Coherent wave sources have the same amplitude.	☐	☐
c) Coherent wave sources produce waves with different frequencies.	☐	☐

Q3 Caleb was listening to a **single note** that his teacher was playing through a loudspeaker. When his teacher connected up another speaker, the sound got **quieter** rather than louder. Explain what was happening to the two sound waves at the place where Caleb was sitting.

....

....

Q4 The diagram shows sets of **overlapping waves** produced by two **dippers** (d1 and d2) in a ripple tank. The **solid** lines indicate where there is a **peak** (or **crest**) and the **dashed** lines indicate where there is a **trough**.

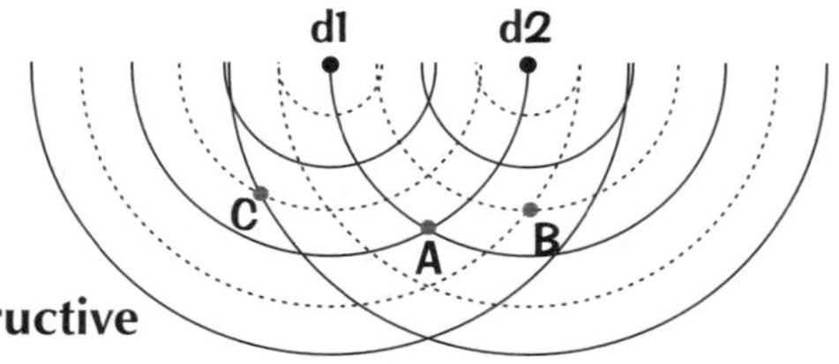

a) For each point A and B decide whether there will be **constructive** or **destructive** interference. Underline the correct answer.

A constructive / destructive **B** constructive / destructive

b) The wavelength of the waves is **1 cm**. Point P is **5 cm** away from d1 and **8 cm** away from d2.

i) What is the **path difference** at point P?

Point P is not on the diagram, by the way.

....

ii) How many **half wavelengths** fit into this path difference?

....

iii) Will there be constructive or destructive **interference** at point P?

....

Diffraction Patterns and Polarisation

Q1 Circle **true** or **false** for each of these statements:

a) Normal light waves are transverse waves vibrating in a mixture of directions. **True / False**

b) Transverse waves can't be plane polarised. **True / False**

c) Plane polarised waves only vibrate in one direction. **True / False**

Q2 **Monochromatic light** was shone onto a screen through **two very thin slits** that were **close together**.

a) **i)** Describe the pattern you would see on the **screen**.

....

ii) Explain why you see this pattern on the screen.

....

....

iii) Explain what this experiment tells you about the nature of light.

....

b) Complete the sentence below about diffraction by circling the correct word.

For a diffraction pattern to occur, the size of the slits must be a **similar / different** size to the wavelength of the light.

Q3 A **laser beam** was projected onto a screen through a pair of **Polaroid sunglasses**. When the glasses were **rotated 90°**, they blocked the light completely.

a) What does this tell you about **laser light**?

....

b) The experiment is repeated using a **torch** instead of a laser. What would you expect to see now when the sunglasses were rotated 90°?

....

....

c) The torch beam is then **reflected** off a glass plate on the bench as shown in the diagram. What happens now when the sunglasses are rotated?

....

....

....

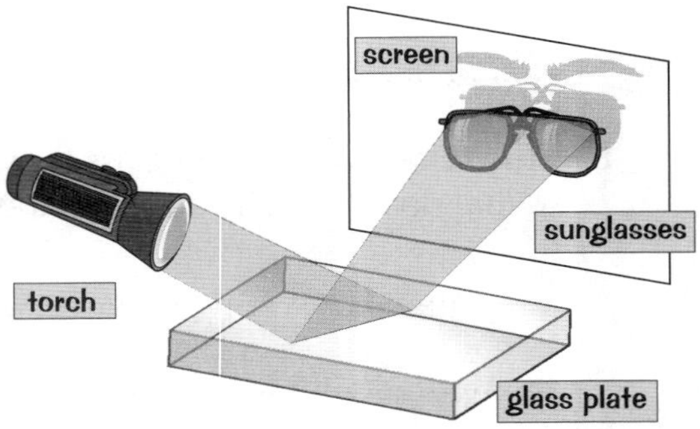

Refraction

Q1 Fill in the **blanks** in the passage below.

> Waves can speed up or .... when they pass from one medium to another. If they are travelling at an angle to the .... then the change in speed can result in a change of ....

Q2 Light is **refracted** when it travels between media with different **densities**.

a) What is meant by a "**normal line**" when talking about **refraction**?

....

b) Circle the correct word(s) in the statements about refraction below.

i) When a wave slows down, it may bend **towards** / **away** from the normal. The wavelength gets **longer** / **shorter** / **stays the same**. The frequency **increases** / **decreases** / **stays the same**.

ii) When a wave speeds up, it may bend **towards** / **away** from the normal. The wavelength gets **longer** / **shorter** / **stays the same**. The frequency **increases** / **decreases** / **stays the same**.

c) On each diagram, draw the ray bending **towards** or **away** from the normal line.

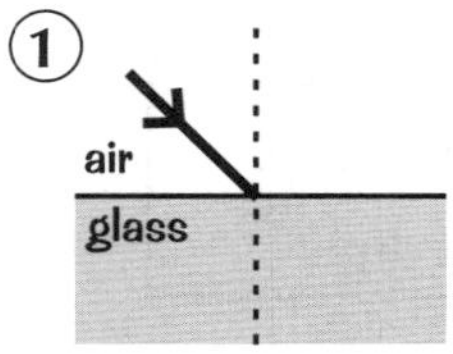

towards normal

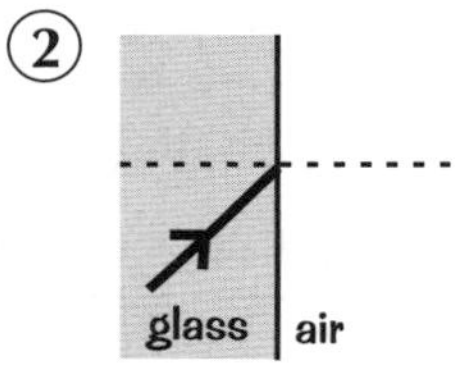

away from normal

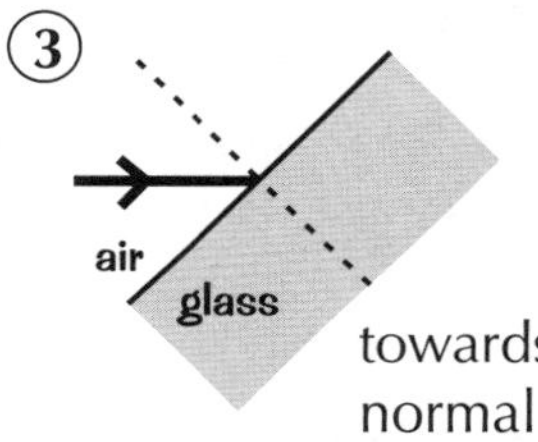

towards normal

d) Describe what is meant by the refractive index of a medium.

....

Q3 The diagram shows **white light** separating into red and violet light when it refracts from air into glass.

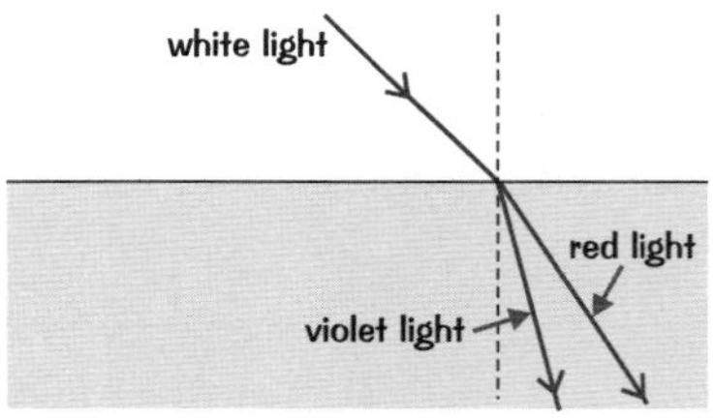

a) The **refractive index** in glass for **red** light is **1.514**. Calculate the speed of red light in a glass block. Speed of light in a vacuum = 3×10^8 m/s.

....

....

b) The refractive index in glass for **violet** light is **1.528**. What does this tell you about the **speed** of violet light in glass compared to red light?

....

....

Refraction: Two Special Cases

Q1 A **prism** can be used to **separate** white light into its **different colours**.

a) What name is given to the **splitting** of white light into different colours?

....

b) Complete the following sentence by circling the correct word.

> Different colours of light are refracted by **different** / **the same** amount(s) in glass because they travel at **different** / **the same** speed(s) in glass.

Q2 Light can bend when it passes from **air** into **glass**.

a) The diagram below shows a ray of **red light** and a ray of **blue light** entering a rectangular **glass block**. **Complete** the diagram by drawing the rays as they **pass completely through** the block (ignoring any reflections).

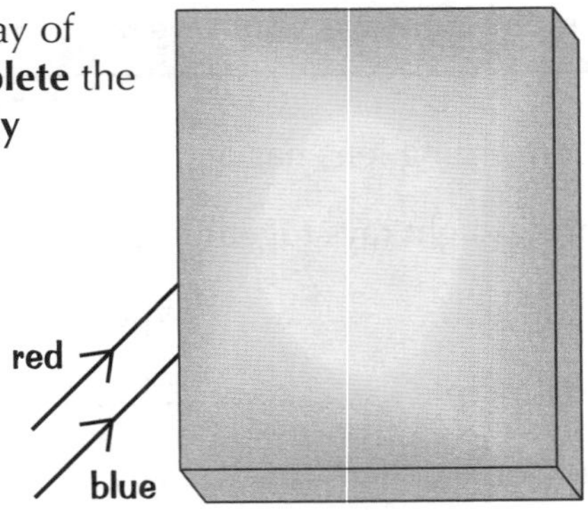

b) Why do the colours of white light noticeably **separate** when they pass through a **triangular** block but not through a **rectangular** one?

Think about what happens as they enter and leave the blocks.

....

....

....

Q3 This question is about **total internal reflection**.

a) What is total internal reflection? Include the term 'critical angle' in your answer.

....

....

b) The **critical angle** for glass/air is **42°**.

Complete the ray diagrams below.

You'll need to measure the angle of incidence for each one — carefully.

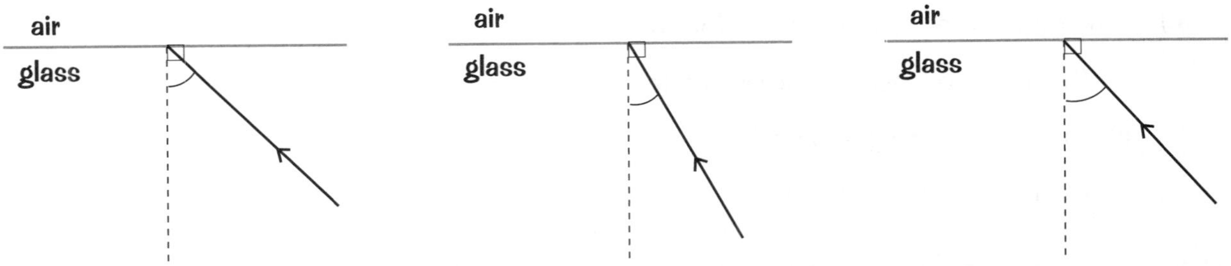

Images and Converging Lenses

Q1 Images can be either **real** or **virtual**.
Tick the appropriate box for each statement below.

	Real	Virtual
a) This kind of image can't be formed on a screen.	☐	☐
b) Light rays only appear to come from this type of image.	☐	☐
c) Light rays actually come from this type of image.	☐	☐
d) This kind of image can be formed on a film.	☐	☐

Q2 Choose from the words below to **complete** the passage.

length concave converges axis parallel turning focal distance convex focus

A converging lens has a .... shape (fatter in the middle than the edges). It brings light rays together (or .... them) to a point called a .... When the rays are .... to each other and to the principle .... of the lens, then the point where the lens brings them together is called the .... point. The distance between the centre of the lens and the focal point is called the focal .... of the lens.

Q3 This lens is forming an **image** on a **screen**.

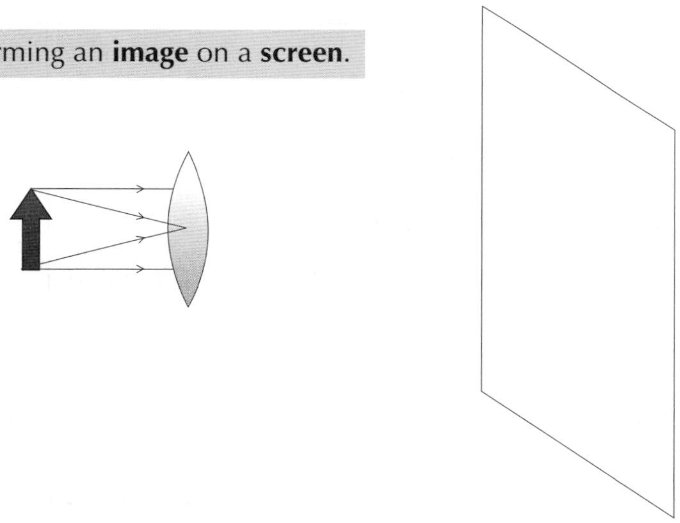

The rays passing through the centre of the lens don't bend.

a) Complete the paths of the rays in the diagram and draw in the image.

b) Circle the correct options in the following sentences.

i) The image is **bigger** / **smaller** than the object.

ii) The image is **upright** / **inverted**.

iii) The image is **real** / **virtual**.

Images and Converging Lenses

Q4 **Convex** lenses are used to **focus light**.

a) On the diagrams below, **label** the following:

Parallel light **Diverging light** **Focal point** **Converging light** **Focal length**

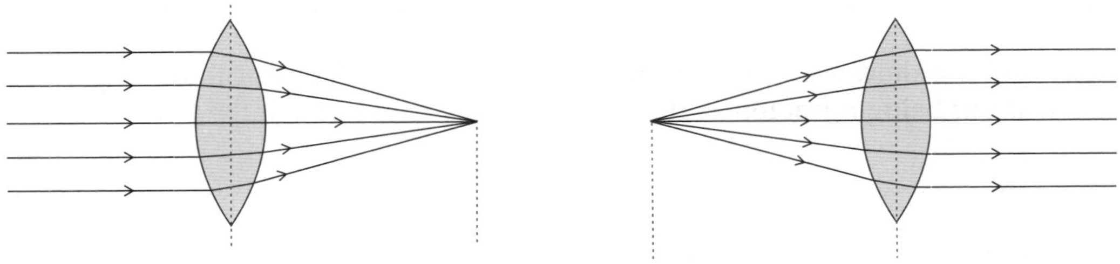

b) On the diagram below, label the following:

Object **Principal axis** **Normal** **Optical centre** **Focal point** **Image**

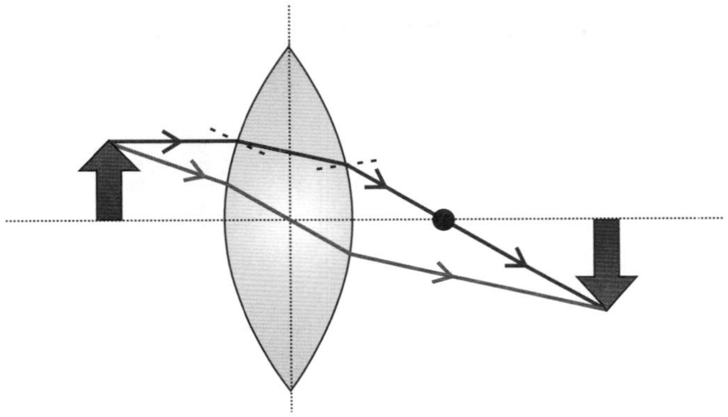

Q5 The diagram below shows another way you can use a **converging** lens to form an **image**.

a) Complete the diagram to show **where** the image is formed.

b) Give a **full description** of the image.

Use the rays that are already there to help you figure it out.

1. ....

2. ....

3. ....

4. ....

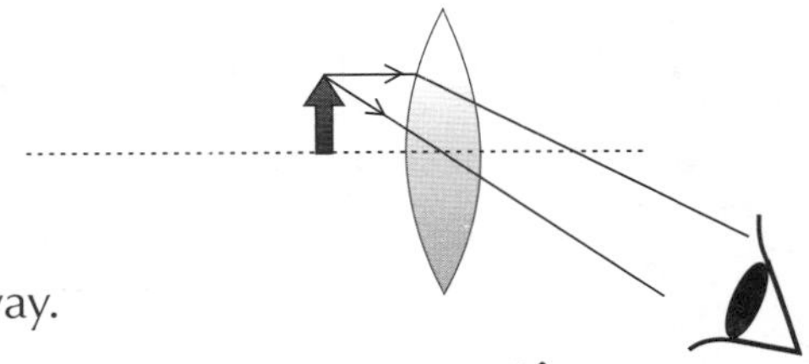

c) Give a possible **application** for this type of lens used in this way.

....

Top Tips: Remember all the things that you need to write down to describe an image formed by a lens. Make sure you can label an image with focal point, focal length, etc. — they might seem like piddly little things but they could be worth a few marks come exam time. It all adds up you know.

Ray Diagrams

Q1 This question is about how to draw **ray diagrams**.

a) The first step is to draw a ray from the top of the object going **parallel** to the axis of the lens. Where does this ray **pass through** when it's **refracted**?

....

b) The next step is to draw a ray from the **top** of the object which passes through the lens **without being refracted**. Where does this ray pass through the lens?

....

c) How do the steps above tell you where the top of the image will be on the **ray diagram**?

....

Q2 **Draw** a ray diagram to locate where the **image** is by following the instructions below.

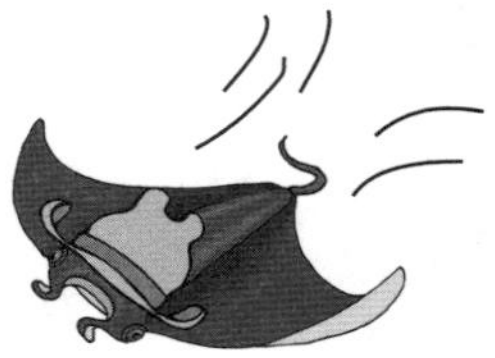

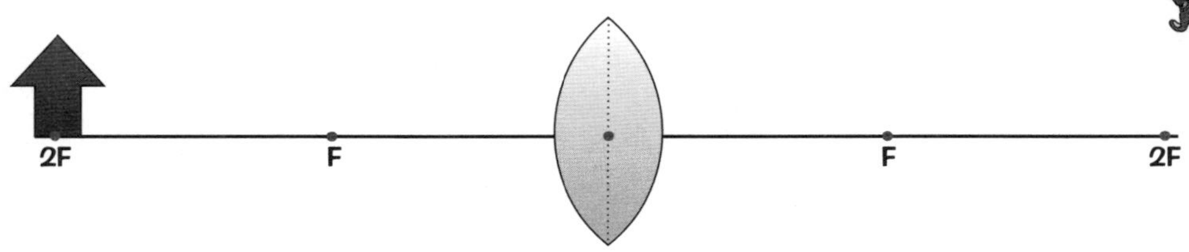

a) Draw a ray from the top of the object (towards the lens) parallel to the axis, and continue the path of the ray through the lens.

b) Draw a ray from the top of the object passing through the centre of the lens.

c) Mark the top of the image.

d) Mark the bottom of the image, and draw in the image.

e) Now describe the image fully.

Do these ray diagrams step by step. Make sure you draw them really carefully, with a ruler.

....

....

....

....

Ray Diagrams

Q3 Complete this ray diagram so that you can **fully describe** the image that this lens produces.

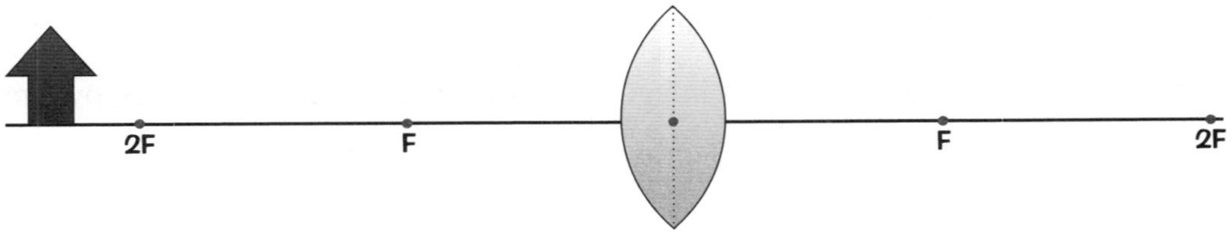

Description of image: ....

....

....

Q4 Complete this ray diagram so that you can fully describe the image that this lens produces.

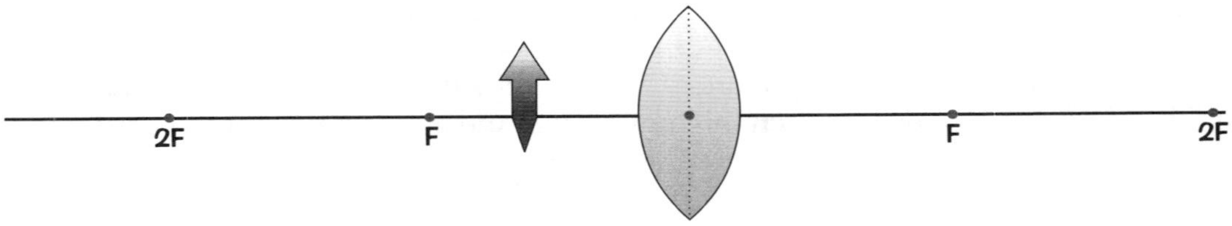

Description of image: ....

....

....

Q5 Here is a **ray diagram** of a lens and an **object** that is **one focal length** away from the lens.

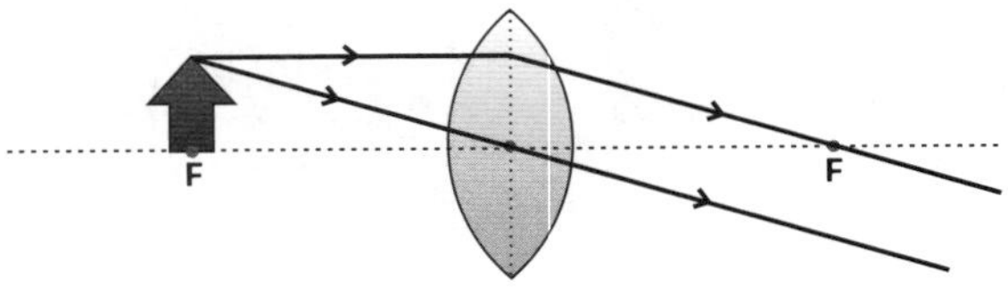

a) How **far away** would the image be? Explain your answer.

Where do these rays meet?

....

....

b) How far away would an object have to be in order to produce an image at the **focal point** on the **right hand side** of the lens?

....

Magnification, Cameras and Projectors

Q1 Convex lenses are used in **cameras** and **projectors**.

a) Describe one **similarity** between an image made by a camera and one made by a projector.

....

b) Describe one **difference** between an image made by a camera and one made by a projector.

....

Q2 The **magnification** of a lens system can be worked out using the **sizes** of the object and the image.

a) Write down the **formula** relating magnification, object size and image size.

....

b) A stamp with a height of **1.5 cm** was observed through a magnifying glass. The virtual image it produced was **6 cm** high. What was the magnification?

....

....

c) A camera was used to take the picture of a tree. If the magnification was **0.002** and the image of the tree was **2 cm** high, what was the actual height of the tree?

....

....

Q3 Complete the ray diagram and take **measurements** to find the **magnification** of this system.

Draw the diagram REALLY carefully.

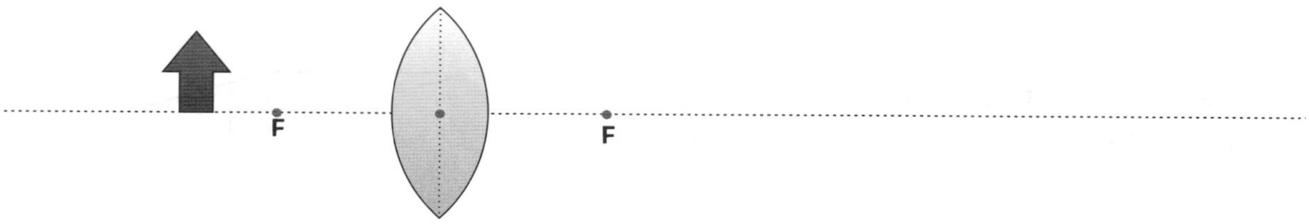

Magnification: ....

....

Magnification, Cameras and Projectors

Q4 **Lenses** are used in **cameras**.

a) Circle the correct word(s) in these statements about a **camera** being used to take a normal family photo.

The magnification is **less than 1** / **exactly 1** / **more than 1**.

The image is **real** / **virtual**.

The image is **upside down** / **the right way up**.

b) Here is a ray diagram for a camera taking a photo of a **flower**.

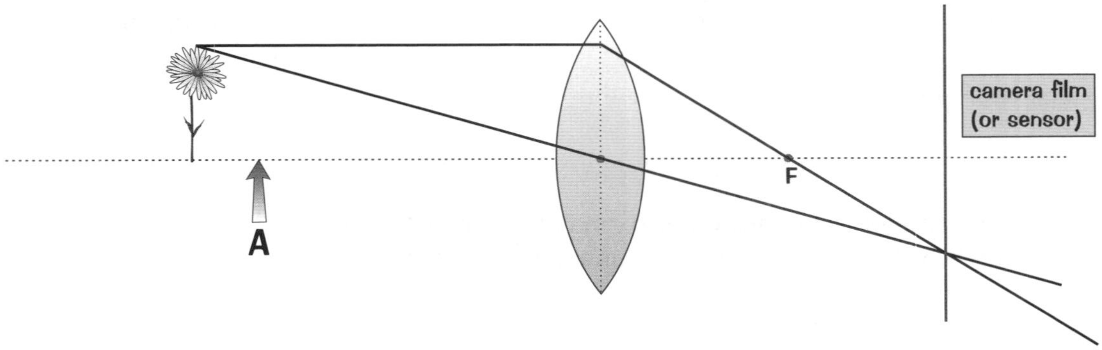

The flower is moved **closer** to the lens as shown by the arrow A in the diagram. Draw in a **new ray diagram** to show where the new image will be.

c) What would you have to do to the camera, to keep the image **focussed** on the film?

....

Q5 This question is about the uses of **lenses** in film **projectors**.

a) Circle the correct word(s) in these statements about lenses in film projectors.

The magnification is **less than 1** / **exactly 1** / **more than 1**.

The image is **real** / **virtual**.

The image is **upside down** / **the right way up**.

b) Which **way up** must the film (the object) go in order to produce the **correct image** on the cinema screen?

....

c) A film projector was moved from one cinema to another cinema where the screen was **further away** from the projector. How should the distance between the film and the lens be changed in order to **focus** the picture correctly on the cinema screen?

....

Mixed Questions — Module P5

Q1 There are **hundreds** of **satellites** orbiting the Earth.

a) The path on the Earth's surface directly beneath a satellite is called its **ground track**. This flattened out map of the Earth shows the ground track of a **polar orbiting satellite**.

On the same diagram, **draw** and **label** a possible ground track of a **geostationary** satellite.

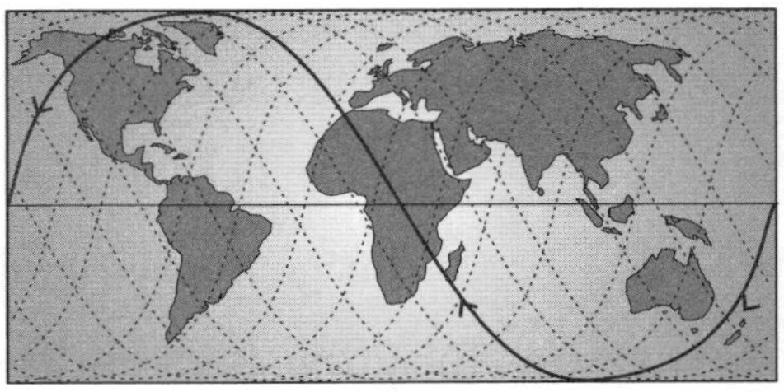

← ground track of polar satellite
— Equator

b) Satellite X is in low polar orbit about **7200 km** away from the centre of the Earth. Geostationary satellites are about **42 000 km** from the centre of the Earth.

i) Satellite X experiences a **centripetal force** of approximately $\mathbf{3.1 \times 10^4}$ **N**. Calculate the force the same satellite would experience if it were in a **geostationary orbit**.

ii) Satellite X completes **one orbit** approximately every **100 minutes**. Calculate its **average speed**, giving your answer in **km/h**.

You'll need to work out the circumference of the orbit.

Q2 Isabel and Josie are having a clarinet lesson with their teacher Mrs Stave. The window is open because it's a hot day. Josie's mum walks past and thinks that the music sounds **muffled**.

a) Use your knowledge of **diffraction** to explain why Josie's mum can't hear the high-pitched sounds.

High-pitched sounds have a higher frequency.

b) Before playing a **duet** Isobel and Josie checked the **tuning** of their instruments.

The girls played the same note, starting at exactly the same time. As Mrs Stave paced up and down the room, she found that the note sounded very loud in some places (**L**) and very quiet in others (**Q**).

Explain why Mrs Stave hears these **differences** in the note as she walks.

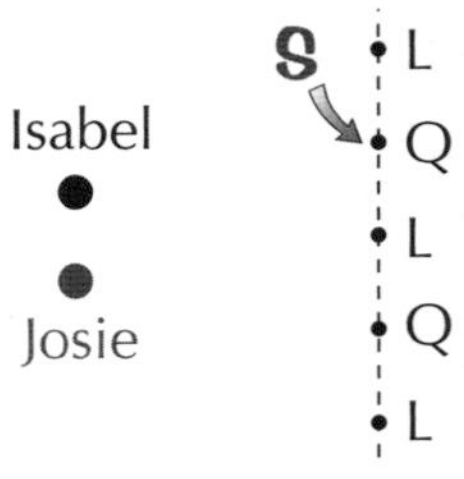

NOT TO SCALE

Think about how the waves are interfering.

Mixed Questions — Module P5

Q3 Anna and Bert are flying their **remote-controlled planes**, as shown.

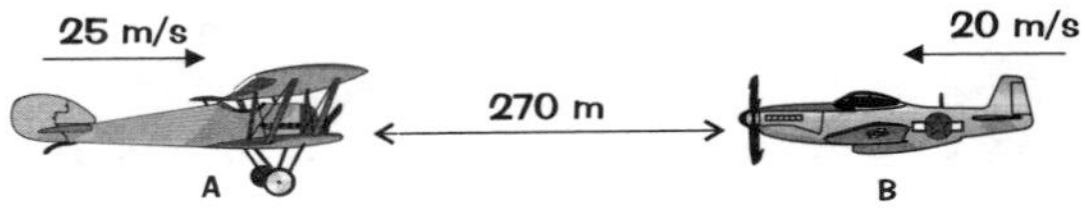

a) What is plane A's **velocity** relative to plane B? .... m/s.

b) Both planes are flying **8 m** above the ground.
If a screw falls off plane A, how long will it take to reach the ground? (Use **g = 10 m/s²**.)

....

....

c) **i)** If the planes continue at the velocities shown, how long would it be before they **collide**?

....

....

ii) Plane A's mass is **600 g**. Plane B's mass is **850 g**. If they collided and stuck together, what would the **horizontal velocities** of the planes be immediately after the collision?

....

....

....

d) Bert directs his plane **upwards** to avert a collision. It is then affected by a wind blowing at **50 km/h north**. His plane was previously flying west at **20 m/s**. Work out its new **speed**.

....

....

....

Q4 The diagram shows light incident on a **bicycle reflector**.

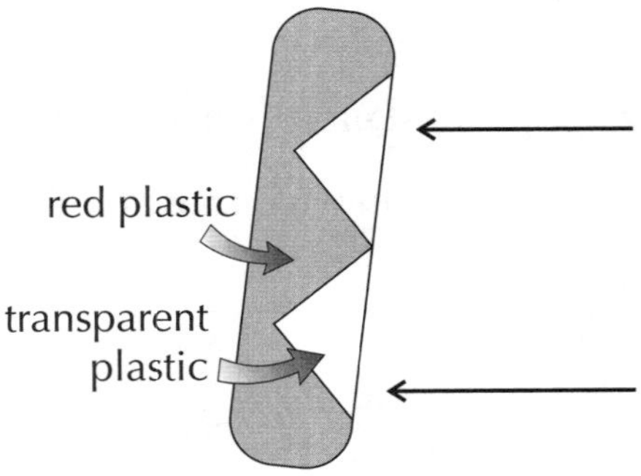

a) Sketch the **paths** of the two light rays after they hit the reflector.

b) The **refractive index** of the transparent plastic is **1.6**.
How **fast** would light travel in the transparent plastic?
(The speed of light in a vacuum is 3×10^8 m/s.)

....

....

....

Circuits and Resistors

Q1 Fill in the **gaps** in the sentences below.

a) The flow of electrons round a circuit is called the ....

b) .... is the 'force' that pushes the current round the circuit.

c) If you increase the voltage, ... current will flow.

d) If you increase the ...., less current will flow.

Q2 Draw circuit **symbols** for each of these components. The first one has been done for you.

a) Ammeter **b)** Switch (open) **c)** Variable resistor **d)** Battery **e)** Bulb

Q3 The diagram shows an old fashioned **variable resistor** with a large **coil of wire** and a sliding **contact**, connected in **series** to a battery and a motor.

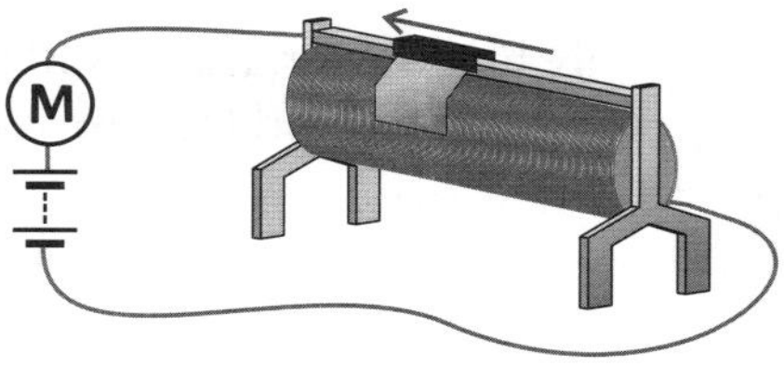

a) Explain **why** the resistance **changes** as you move the contact.

....

....

....

b) i) How would the **resistance** of the variable resistor change if you moved the contact to the **left** (as shown)?

....

ii) What would happen to the **speed** of the motor if you moved the contact to the **left** (as shown)?

....

Q4 **Resistance** reduces the flow of current in a circuit.

a) Explain what **causes resistance** in a metal conductor.

....

....

....

b) What **increases** as resistance increases in a metal conductor?

....

Voltage-Current Graphs and Resistors

Q1 Circle the correct words in the following statements.

a) The resistance of a filament lamp **increases** / **decreases** as it gets hotter.

b) The steeper the gradient of a V-I graph, the **higher** / **lower** the resistance is.

c) The current through a resistor at constant temperature is **directly** / **inversely** proportional to the voltage.

Q2 The graph below shows **V-I curves** for four **resistors**.

Gradient = $\frac{\text{vertical change}}{\text{horizontal change}}$

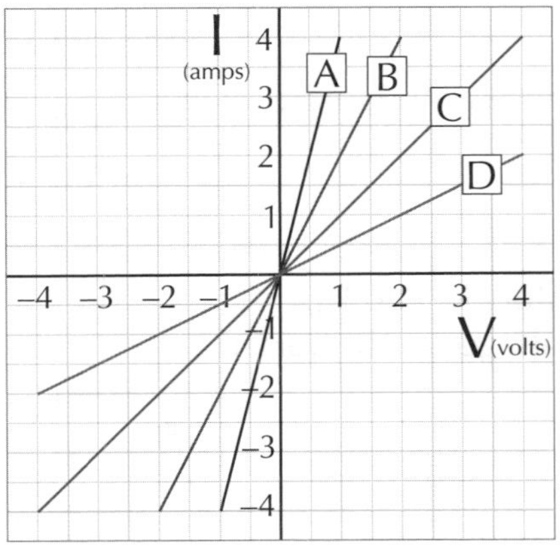

a) Which resistor has the **highest** resistance? ....

b) Calculate the **gradient** of the line for resistor B.

....

c) Calculate the **resistance** of resistor B.

....

Q3 The graph shows a V-I curve for a **filament lamp**.

Explain why the graph **curves**.

Think about what happens to the filament of the lamp when it has a large voltage across it.

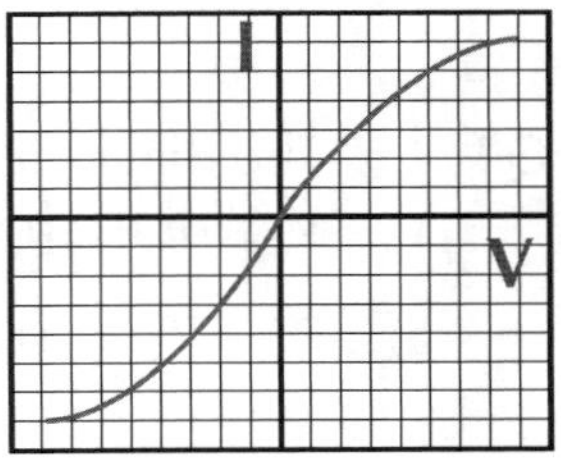

....

....

....

....

Q4 **Resistors** can be connected together in a circuit in **series** or in **parallel**.

a) How does connecting resistors in parallel rather than in series affect the **total resistance** of a circuit?

....

b) Complete the circuit diagram on the right by connecting the resistors in **parallel**.

c) **Calculate** the total resistance in the circuit on the right.

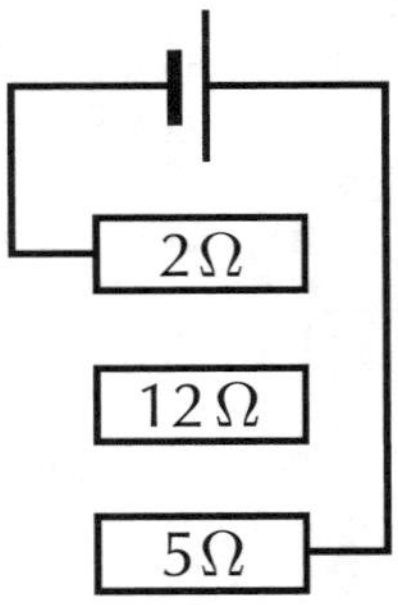

....

....

....

Potential Dividers

Q1 Complete the sentences by **circling** the correct **word** or **words**.

a) A potential divider consists of a **single resistor** / **pair of resistors**.

b) They **multiply** / **divide** the voltage in a circuit.

c) The higher the resistance the **bigger** / **smaller** the voltage drop across it.

Q2 Tick to show whether the following statements are **true** or **false**.

		True	False
a)	The voltage at the point between the resistors is the output of the potential divider.	☐	☐
b)	The output voltage can have any value.	☐	☐
c)	If the resistors are equal then the output voltage will be 50% of the total voltage.	☐	☐
d)	To vary the output, both the resistors must be variable resistors.	☐	☐

Q3 The diagram shows a **potential divider** consisting of resistors R_1 and R_2. Complete the statements below about how the **output voltage** can be **varied**.

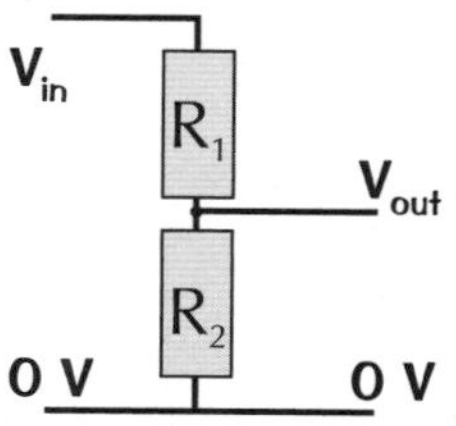

a) If the output voltage is too **low** you could increase it by

.... the resistance of resistor $\mathbf{R_1}$.

b) If the output voltage is too **high** you could decrease it by

.... the resistance of resistor ....

Q4 The diagram shows a potential divider. Calculate the output voltage V_{out} for each of the following **sets** of values for $\mathbf{R_1}$ and $\mathbf{R_2}$.

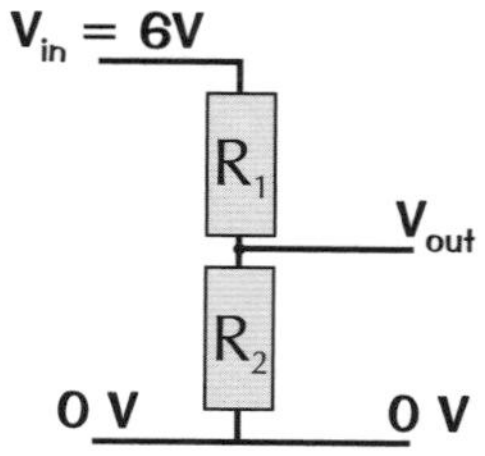

a) $R_1 = R_2 = 10\ \Omega$. ....

....

b) $R_1 = 20\ \Omega$. $R_2 = 10\ \Omega$. ....

....

c) $R_1 = 10\ \Omega$. $R_2 = 20\ \Omega$. ....

....

Q5 A **pair** of resistors, R_1 and R_2, makes up a potential divider. The total **input** voltage is **6 V**. The graph shows how the output voltage changes as R_1 is changed.

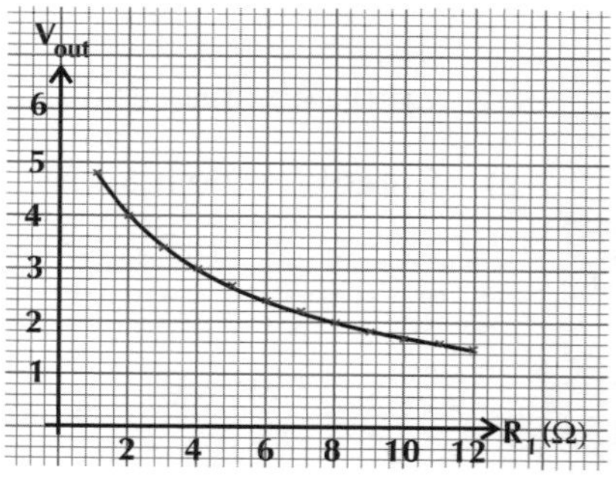

a) What value of R_1 gives an output voltage of **2.2 V**? ....

b) What value of R_1 gives an output voltage of **6.0 V**? ....

c) Use the graph to find the value of R_2.

....

LDRs and Thermistors

Q1 Cross out the incorrect word from each pair to make the following statements **true**.

a) An LDR has a high resistance in very **bright** / **dim** light.

b) A thermistor gets **more** / **less** resistive as the temperature drops.

Q2 After each sentence, write **LDR**, **thermistor**, or **both** as appropriate.

a) Changes its resistance in response to conditions around it. ....

b) Could be used as part of a thermostat. ....

c) Would have a high resistance in a warm dark room. ....

d) Would have a low resistance in a warm dark room. ....

Q3 A motor rotates the blades of a **fan**. The motor is in **series** with an **LDR** as shown in this circuit diagram.

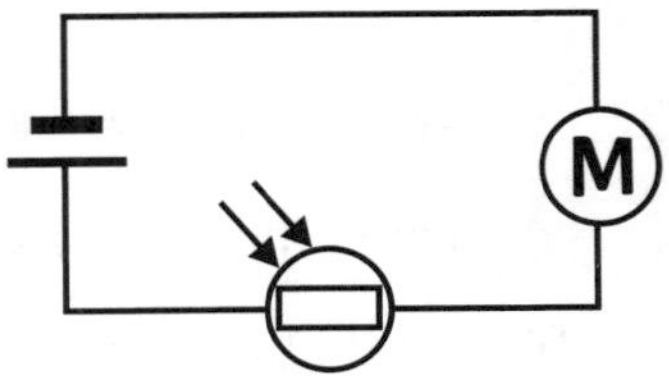

a) What happens to the **speed** of the fan as the light in the room **fades**?

....

b) Why does this happen?

....

....

....

Q4 An electrical **thermometer** includes the potential divider shown.

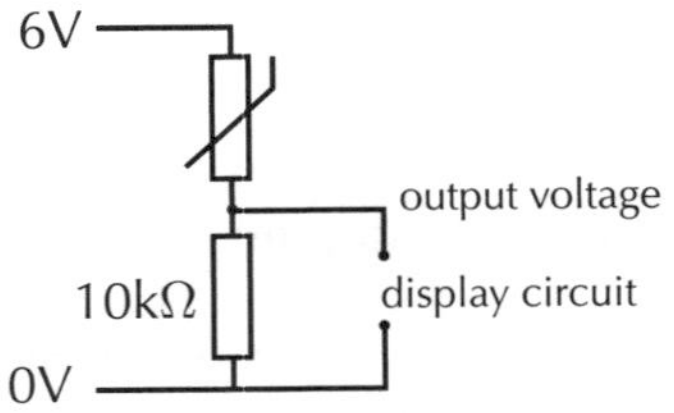

a) At 30°C the resistance of the thermistor is **10 kΩ**. What would the **output voltage** be at 30°C?

....

b) What would happen to the **resistance** of the thermistor if the room got **warmer**?

....

c) What would happen to the **output voltage** if the room got **colder**?

....

d) What would happen to the **output voltage** if the room got **colder** and the thermistor was in the $\mathbf{R_2}$ position instead?

....

Transistors

Q1 Use **five** of the words provided to **label** the circuit below, which is used to control an **LED**.

transistor

LED

voltmeter

high resistor

switch

thermistor

ammeter

power supply

variable resistor

ohmmeter

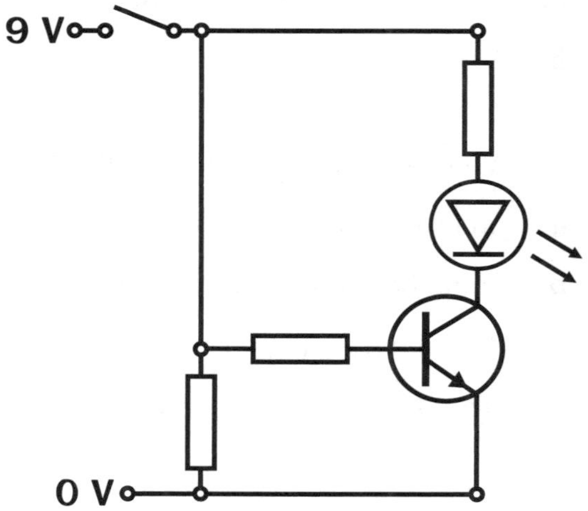

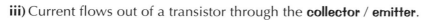

Q2 **Transistors** are the basic **building blocks** of many electronic components.

a) Label the base (**B**), collector (**C**) and emitter (**E**) on the circuit symbol of an npn transistor below:

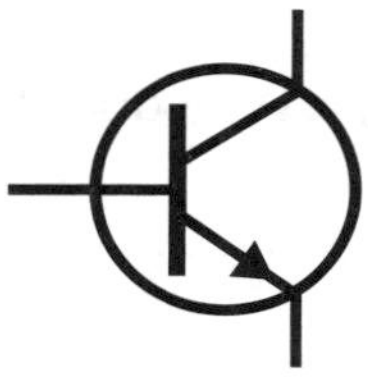

b) Circle the **correct** words in the following statements:

i) When there is no current passing through the base of a transistor a current **can** / **cannot** flow through the rest of the transistor.

ii) Current flows into a transistor through the **collector** / **emitter**.

iii) Current flows out of a transistor through the **collector** / **emitter**.

c) Give **one** example of an electronic component made using transistors.

....

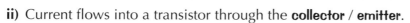

Q3 The **circuit diagram** below shows a simple circuit that contains a **transistor**.

a) When the switch is **open** (as shown) ammeter A_1 shows a reading of **0 A**. What will be the reading on ammeter A_2?

....

b) The switch is **closed**. A_1 now has a reading of **0.08 A** and A_2 has a reading of **2.3 A**. Calculate the reading on A_3.

....

....

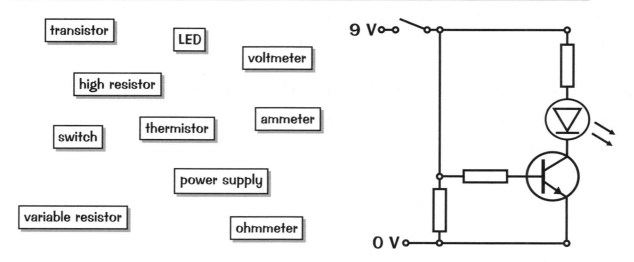

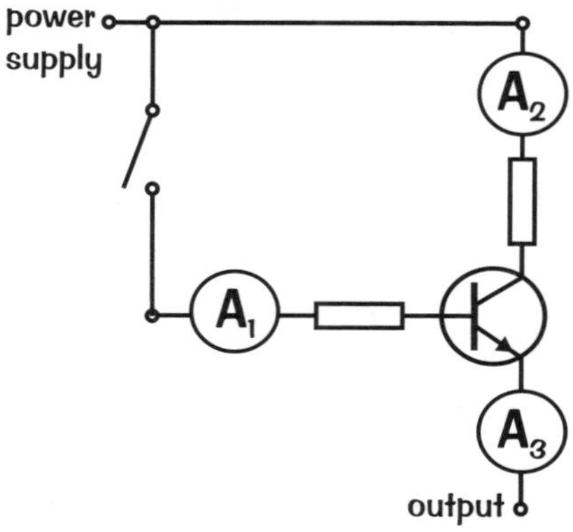

Top Tips: Transistors are super-handy and I wouldn't want to live without them. However, it can be pretty tricky to get your head around how they actually work. So get yourself comfortable in your base, apply some practice and collect the information so that you're ready to emit it in the exam.

Logic Gates

Q1 Fill in the gaps in the following sentences about **logic gates**.

a) An electronic system in which the only possible values are on and off is described as a .... system.

b) A NOT gate is sometimes called an ....

c) The five main kinds of logic gate are ....

Q2 Write the correct **component name** under each **symbol**.

a) **b)** **c)** **d)** **e)**

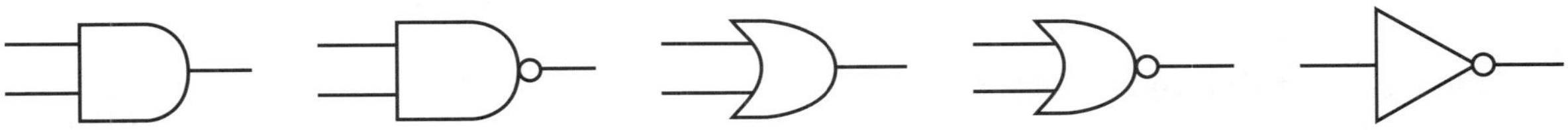

a) .... b) .... c) .... d) .... e) ....

Q3 For each of the following descriptions, write down the **name** of the **logic gate** which **fits**.

a) Output is 0 unless both inputs are 0. ....

b) Only has one input. Output is 1 if input is 0. ....

c) The only time output is 1 is when both inputs are 1. ....

d) Output is 1 unless both inputs are 1. ....

Q4 What kind of **logic gate** would give each of the **truth tables** below? Write the correct **name** of the logic gate under each truth table.

A	B	Output
0	0	1
0	1	0
1	0	0
1	1	0

....

A	B	Output
0	0	0
0	1	0
1	0	0
1	1	1

....

A	B	Output
0	0	1
0	1	1
1	0	1
1	1	0

....

in	out
0	1
1	0

....

Q5 Peter draws a truth table for a **NAND** gate. He makes **mistakes**.

A	B	Output
0	0	0
0	1	1
1	0	1
1	1	1

a) **Correct** his mistakes in the table.

b) What **combination** of two gates would be the **same** as a NAND gate?

There's a clue in the name of the NAND logic gate.

.... then ....

Using Logic Gates

Q1 This diagram shows a **logic circuit**.

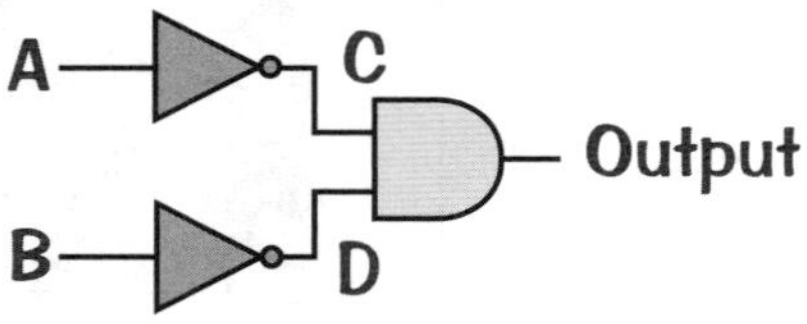

A	B	C	D	Output
0	0			
1	0			
0	1			
1	1			

Marie thinks that this logic circuit might be the same as a **NOR** gate. She plans a **truth table** to prove it:

a) Finish the truth table by inserting all the **missing values**.

b) Was Marie's idea correct — is this circuit the same as a NOR gate? ....

Q2 **AND** logic gates give an output of 1 if **both** inputs are 1.

Use the circuit symbols given in the box to complete the circuit diagram for an AND logic gate.

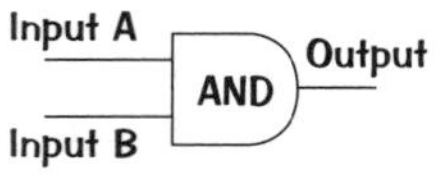

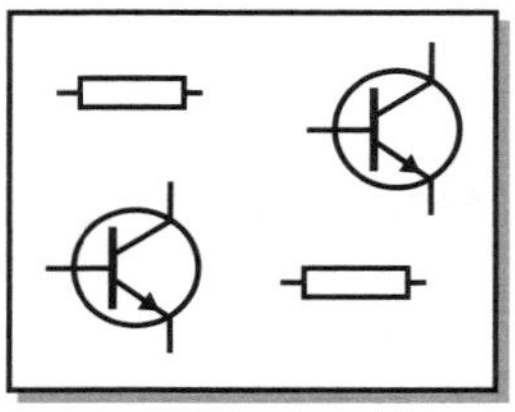

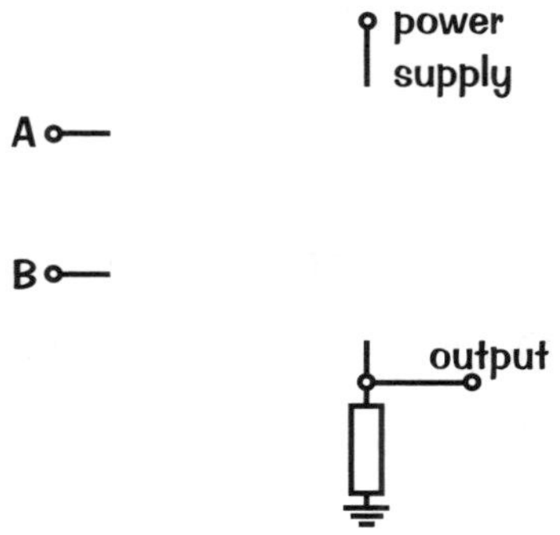

Q3 Mr Green's shop has three doors.
He wants a bell to **ring** if any door **opens**.

He designs the following logic circuit.

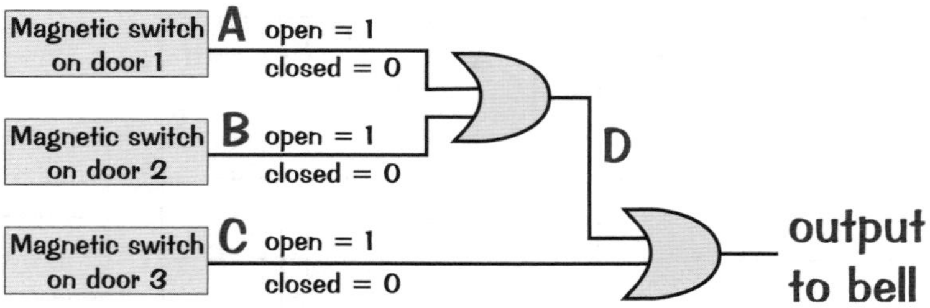

A	B	C	D	Output
0	0	0		
0	0	1		
0	1	0		
0	1	1		
1	0	0		
1	0	1		
1	1	0		
1	1	1		

a) Complete the truth table for the logic circuit.

b) Will the bell ring when **any** one door is opened? ....

c) Mr Green installs a switch (**S**) which he wants to use to turn the bell circuit **on** and **off**.

Mr Green turns the switch **off** and finds that the bell **still rings** when a door is **opened**. Explain why this happens.

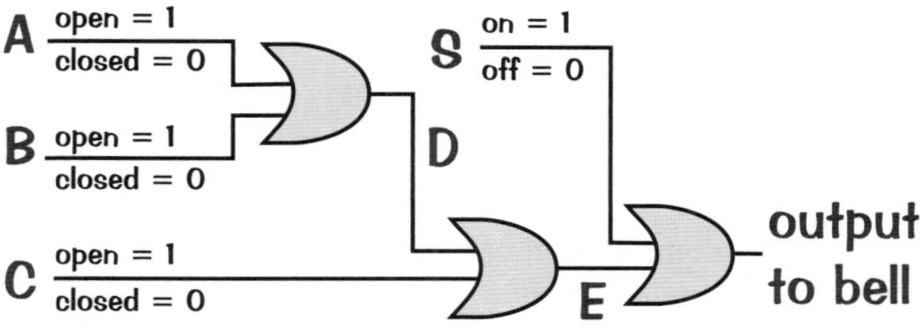

....

....

LEDs and Relays in Logic Circuits

Q1 Indicate whether the following statements are **true** or **false**.

		True	False
a)	Current can only flow one way through an LED.	☐	☐
b)	LEDs need a large current to work.	☐	☐
c)	An LED uses very little power.	☐	☐

Q2 LEDs can be used to show the **output** of a logic gate.

Write down **two** reasons why **LEDs** rather than ordinary **lamp bulbs** are used in logic circuits.

1. ....

2. ....

Q3 Logic gates are often used to switch devices **on** and **off**.

a) Explain why logic gates can't be used to switch devices on and off in **high current** circuits.

....

b) Suggest how a logic circuit could be used to switch on a **starter motor**, even though the starter motor needs a high current.

....

....

Q4 A relay uses an **electromagnet** to connect two circuits.

a) Explain how the logic circuit shown in the diagram can switch the high-current circuit **on** and **off**.

....

....

....

....

....

....

....

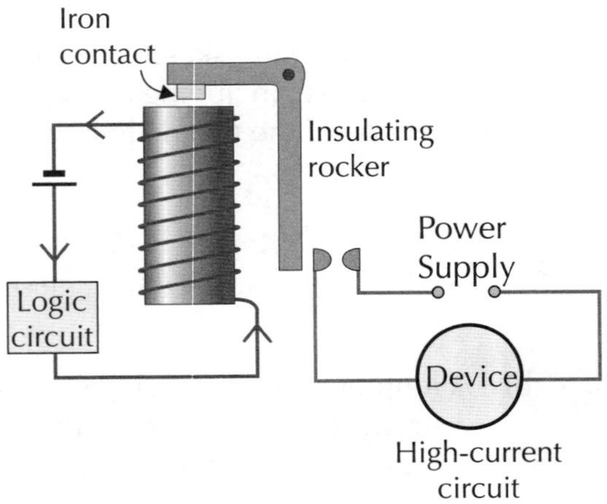

b) Describe a benefit of using a **relay** to switch on a device which requires a **large current**.

....

....

Magnetic Fields

Q1 Fill in the word **North** or **South** in the following sentences.

a) A .... pole will repel a North pole.

b) Field lines always point towards a .... pole.

c) Reversing the current in a solenoid will turn a .... pole into a South pole.

d) A .... pole is found when a current appears to go clockwise in a coil.

Q2 Tick to show whether the following are **true** or **false**. Write a **correct** version of each false statement.

		True	False
a)	Inside a coil the magnetic field is just like a bar magnet.	☐	☐
b)	Iron keeps its magnetism when the current is switched off.	☐	☐
c)	As more turns are added to a coil its magnetic field gets weaker.	☐	☐
d)	Adding a soft iron core will increase the strength of the solenoid's magnetic field.	☐	☐

Q3 The diagram below shows a **wire** carrying a current passing through a piece of **flat card**.

a) Some **iron filings** are sprinkled onto the card. When the current is switched on, a **pattern** develops in the iron filings.

On the diagram, **sketch** the pattern the iron filings make, including **arrows** to show the direction of the magnetic field.

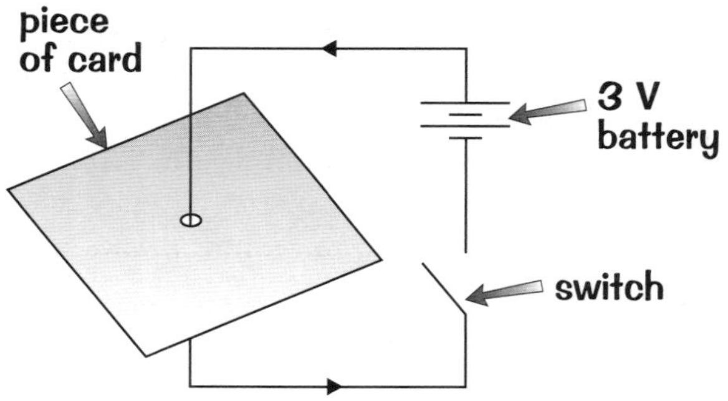

Remember the direction of conventional current flow. Then use your hand...

b) A **loop** of current-carrying wire (shown on the right) has a **stronger** magnetic field **inside** the loop than outside. Explain why this is, including a sketch of the magnetic field.

....

....

....

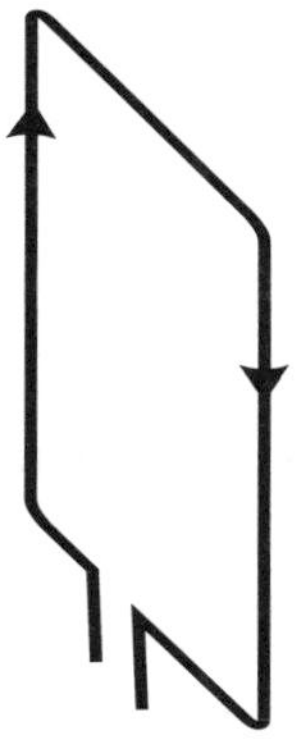

Magnetic Fields

Q4 The diagram below shows a **coil** of wire carrying a current (a **solenoid**).

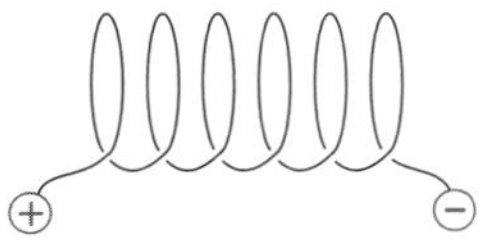

a) Draw the **shape** of the **magnetic field** in and around the coil.

b) Indicate on the diagram the **North** and **South** poles of the solenoid.

c) What effect would the solenoid have on a piece of **soft iron** placed near one of its ends?

....

d) Sarah holds a **bar magnet** with its North pole nearest to the left hand end of the coil in the diagram. The bar magnet experiences a **force**.

i) In what **direction** would the force on the bar magnet be — **towards** the coil or **away** from it?

....

ii) Suggest **two** different ways in which the direction of this force could be **reversed**.

....

....

Q5 Explain why the following are **bad ideas**.

a) Using your **left hand** to work out the direction of a **magnetic field** around a **current carrying wire**.

....

....

b) Reversing the current in **both** of a pair of solenoids to stop them repelling each other.

....

....

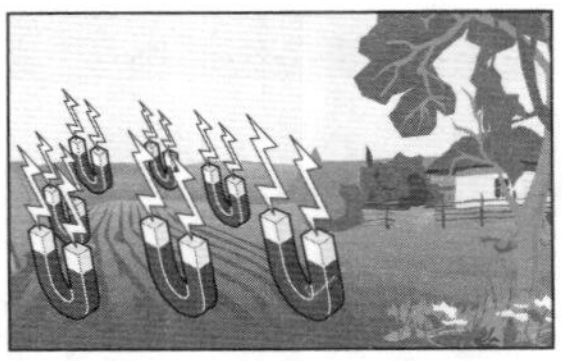

Top Tips: Make sure you always draw magnetic field arrows going the right way. It's easy to lose marks on fiddly bits like that when you aren't paying attention. And don't go using the wrong hand to work out the field around a current-carrying wire — cos you'll get it wrong if you do that.

The Motor Effect

Q1 Complete the passage below using the words supplied.

force	field	angle	stronger	permanent	current	magnetic	magnets

A wire carrying an electric current has a ....

around it. This can interact with the magnetic fields of other wires or of ....

.... to produce a .... and sometimes movement.

A bigger .... or a .... magnet will produce a bigger force.

Q2 The diagram shows an electrical wire between **two magnetic poles**. When the current is switched on, the wire **moves** at right angles to the magnetic field.

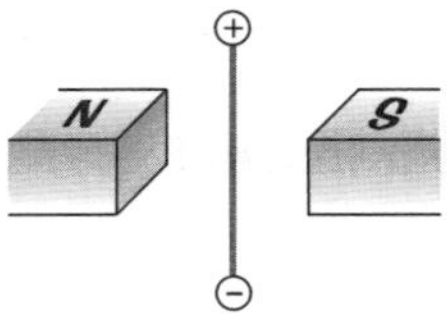

Use Fleming's LHR.

a) Which way will the wire **move**?

....

b) How could the wire be made to move in the **opposite** direction? ....

c) Explain **why** the wire moves.

....

....

Q3 This experiment was set up to illustrate the **motor effect**. When the current is switched on the bar rolls along the rails.

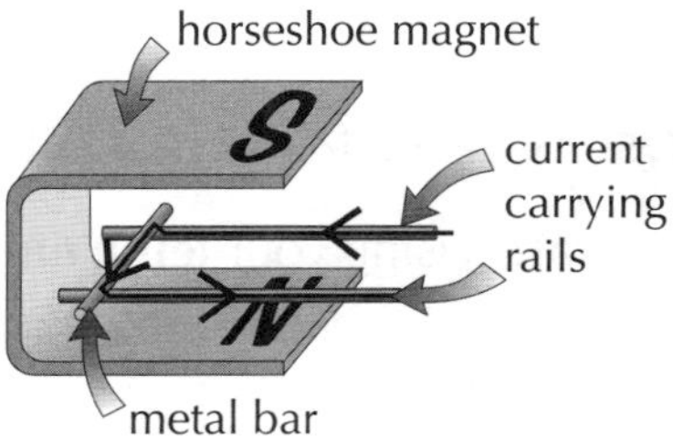

a) Which of the statements **A** to **D** below states correctly what the experiment shows? Circle the appropriate letter.

A A force acts in the same direction as the current is flowing.
B The magnetic field from the magnet combining with the field from the current in the bar.
C The horseshoe magnet pushing the bar along.
D The current in the bar pulling it along the rails.

b) Give **two changes** you could make to the experiment to:

i) **reverse the direction** of the force on the bar.

....

....

ii) **increase the magnitude** of the force on the bar.

....

....

The Simple Electric Motor

Q1 Which of the following will make an electric motor spin **faster**? Circle the relevant letter(s).

- **A** Having more turns on the coil.
- **B** Using a stronger magnetic field.
- **C** Using a soft iron core.
- **D** Using a bigger current.
- **E** Using a commutator.

Q2 Read the three statements below. Tick the box next to each statement that you think is **true**.

- ☐ The split ring commutator makes the motor spin faster.
- ☐ The split ring commutator reverses the direction of the current every half turn by swapping the contacts to the DC supply.
- ☐ The split ring commutator reverses the polarity of the DC supply every half turn.

Q3 The diagram shows a current-carrying **coil** in a magnetic field.

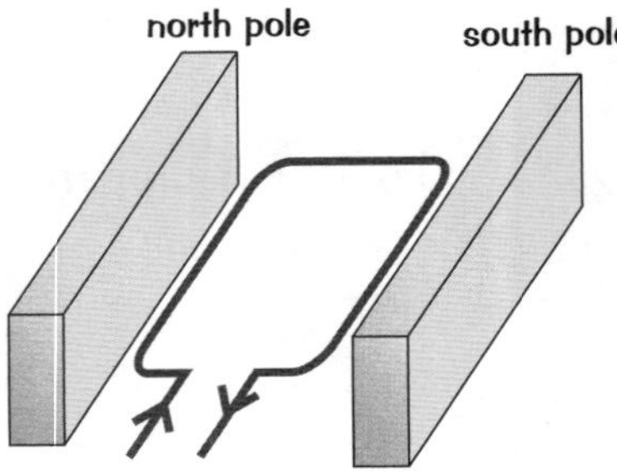

a) Draw an arrow on the diagram to show the **direction** of the magnetic field.

b) Describe the direction of the force on the **left-hand arm** of the coil.

....

c) In which direction will the coil **move** — **clockwise** or **anticlockwise**? ....

d) This diagram shows the coil just after it has turned through 90°. Draw arrows to show the direction of the forces on **each arm** of the coil at this stage and describe how you would expect the coil to **move**.

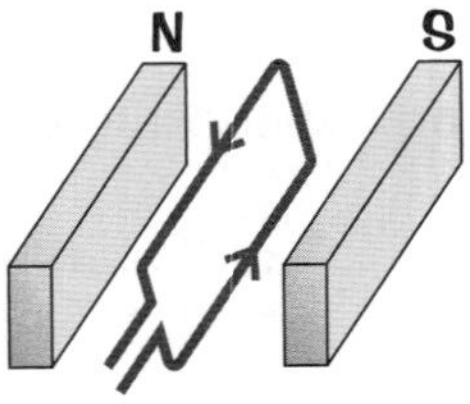

....

e) In a motor, the coil keeps rotating in the **same direction**. Explain how this is achieved.

....

....

....

f) In a practical motor, the poles of the magnet are strongly **curved**. Explain why.

....

....

....

Electromagnetic Induction

Q1 a) Write down a definition of **electromagnetic induction**.

..

..

b) What is **another** name for electromagnetic induction?

..

Q2 Tick the boxes to show whether the following are **true** or **false**.

	True	False
a) You can induce a voltage in a wire by moving the wire back and forth near a magnet.	☐	☐
b) You can induce a voltage in a wire by moving a magnet back and forth near a wire.	☐	☐
c) If you keep moving a wire back and forth in a magnetic field you will get a DC current.	☐	☐
d) The faster you move a wire back and forth in a magnetic field, the higher the voltage.	☐	☐

Q3 Look at the **apparatus** shown in the diagram.

Happiness-reading ammeter

Centre-reading ammeter

Electrical wire

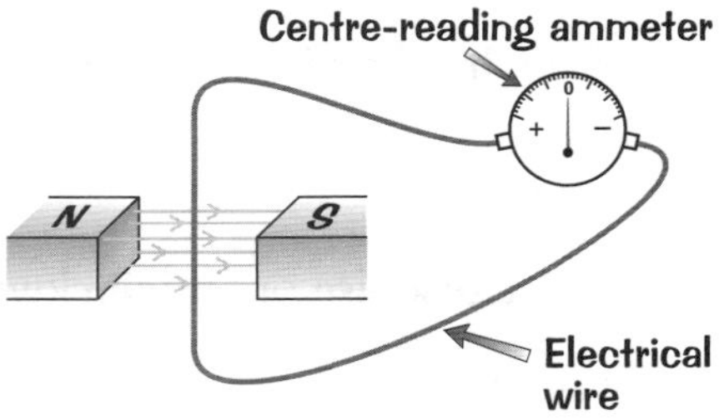

a) Describe how you could use the apparatus to demonstrate **electromagnetic induction**.

..

..

b) What you would see on the **ammeter**?

..

..

c) What effect, if any, would the following have:

i) swapping the magnetic poles?

..

ii) reversing the connections to the ammeter?

..

Electromagnetic Induction

Q4 The diagram shows a **hamster-powered dynamo**.

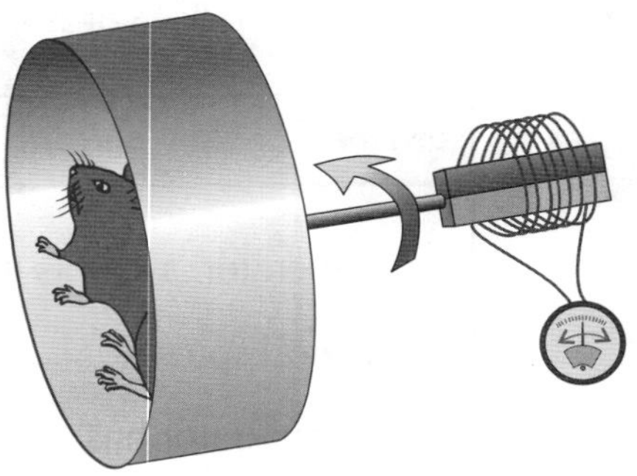

a) What happens in the coil of wire when the hamster runs at a **constant speed**? Explain your answer.

....

....

....

b) What would change if the hamster ran in the **opposite direction** (at the same speed as before)?

....

c) What would change if the hamster ran at a **higher speed** in the same direction as in part **a)**?

....

....

Q5 Moving a magnet inside an electric coil produces a **trace** on a cathode ray **oscilloscope**.

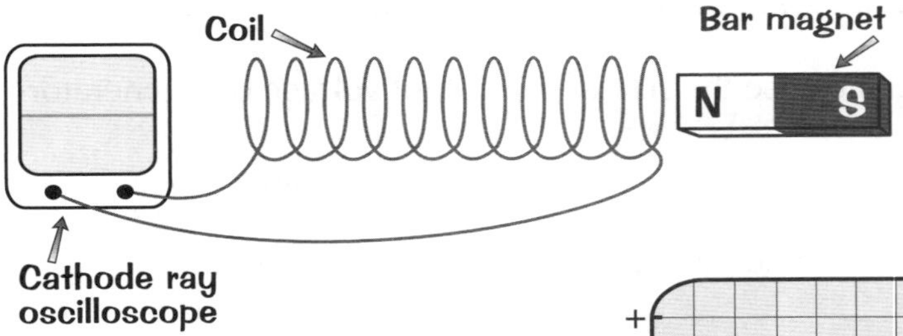

When the magnet is pushed **into** the coil in 2 seconds it produces the trace on the right.

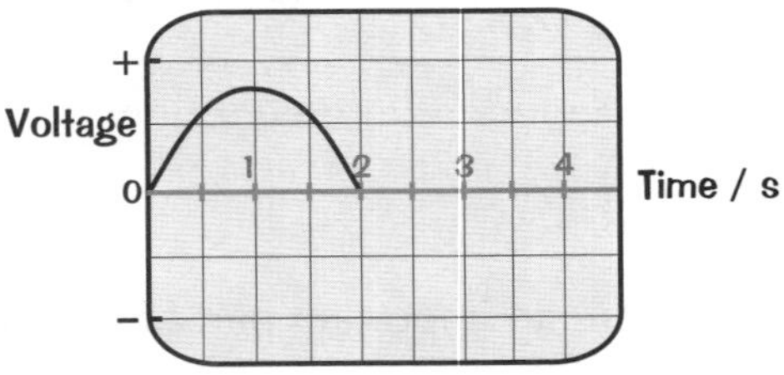

Draw the trace produced when:

a) the magnet is pushed into and pulled out of the coil in 4 seconds, at the same speed as above.

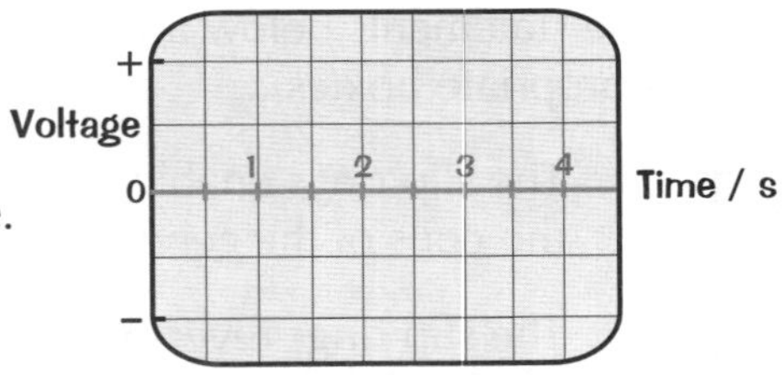

b) the magnet is pushed into and pulled out of the coil repeatedly, twice as fast as above.

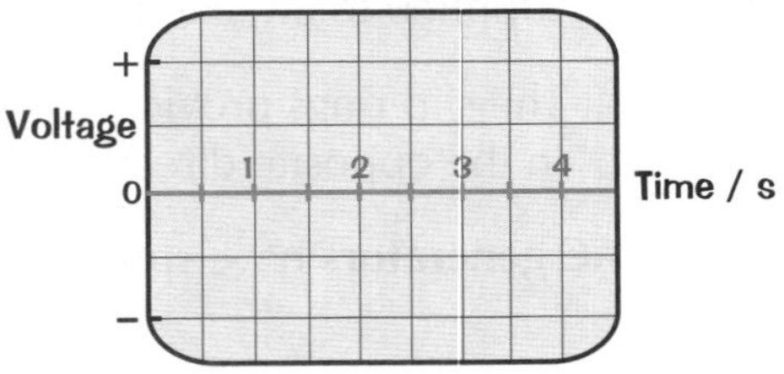

Top Tips: Some of this will be familiar from module P2. It's worth making doubly sure you know it, because you might get harder exam questions on it for this module than for P2. Be prepared.

Generators

Q1 Choose from the words below to complete the passage.

brushes	field	current	direction	drier	half	full	motors	slip	split	magnetic	tumble

In a generator, a coil is made to turn inside a ....
As the coil spins a .... is induced in it. Instead of a split ring commutator, an AC generator has .... rings and .... AC generators produce current which changes .... every .... turn.

Q2 **Generators** are used in **power stations** to produce electricity.

a) What **rotates** in a generator in a power station?

....

b) What **type of current** does a generator in a power station generate?

....

c) **i)** How could you increase the **size** of the output **voltage** of a generator?

....

ii) How could you increase the **frequency** of the output voltage of a generator?

....

Q3 **Slip-rings** are an important part of generators.

a) Which of the statements below about slip rings in a generator are **true**? Tick the appropriate box(es).

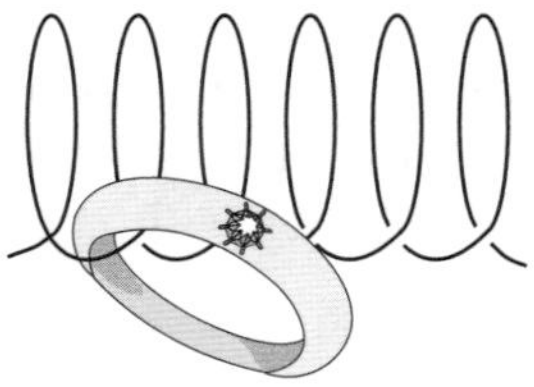

☐ The slip rings enable the current to enter and leave the coils of the generator while it is turning.

☐ The slip rings reverse the direction of the current supplied to an external circuit every half turn.

☐ The slip rings provide current to an external circuit in the opposite direction every full turn.

b) Why don't **AC generators** have split-ring commutators? *Think about what split-ring commutators do.*

....

....

Generators

Q4 Here is a **CRO** display of the **voltage** produced by a generator.

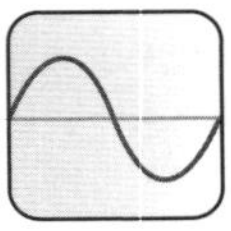

The displays below show the voltage produced under **different conditions**.

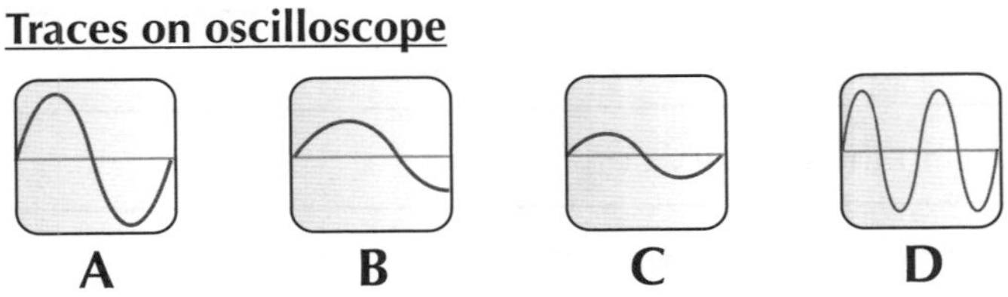

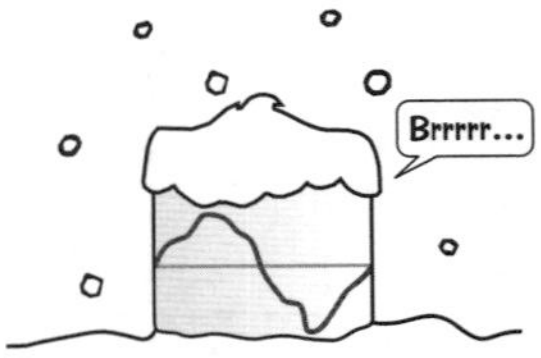

A trace in cold conditions.

Pick the correct letter **A-D** to show:

a) The generator turning **twice as fast**. ....

b) The generator turning more **slowly** than originally. ....

c) The generator turning at the **same speed** as originally but with **stronger magnets**. ....

Q5 Here is another CRO display of the **voltage** produced by an **AC generator**.

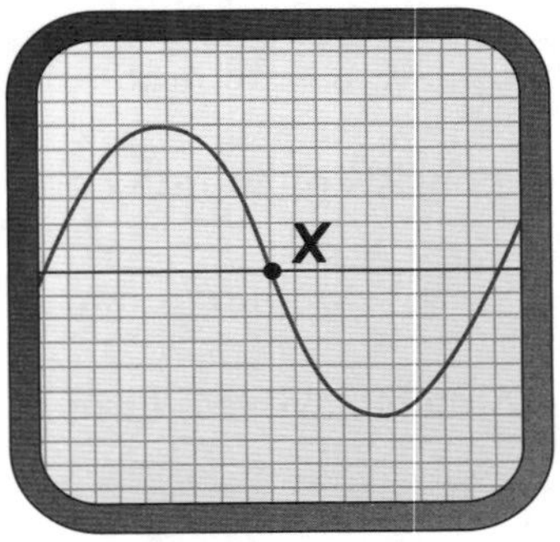

Point **X** on the diagram happened when the coil was like this in the magnetic field:

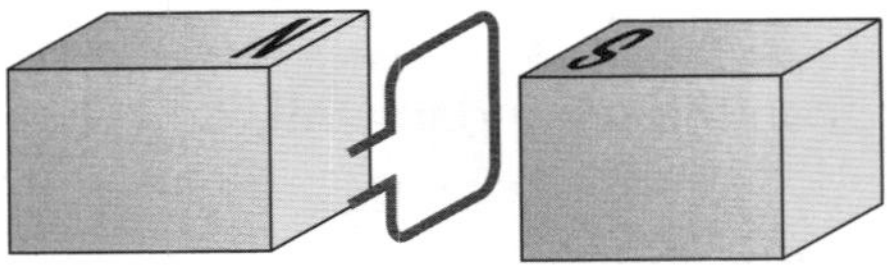

a) Mark the letter **Y** on the diagram of the display to show another point when the coil is in a **similar position**.

This diagram shows the coil in another position in the magnetic field.

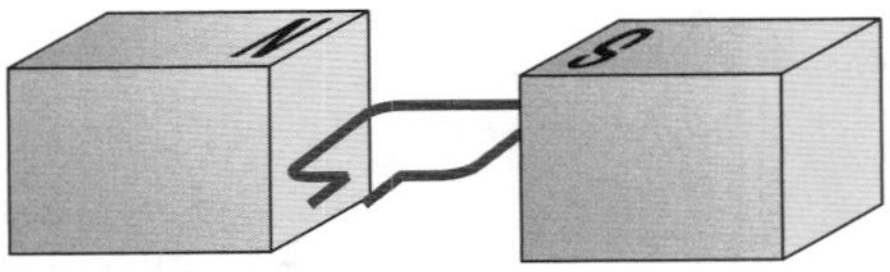

Think about how much the position of the coil has changed.

b) Mark the letter **Z** on the diagram of the display above to show a point where the coil is like this in the magnetic field.

c) On the CRO screen to the right, draw a trace to show how the voltage would **change** if the generator's slip rings were changed for a split ring **commutator**.

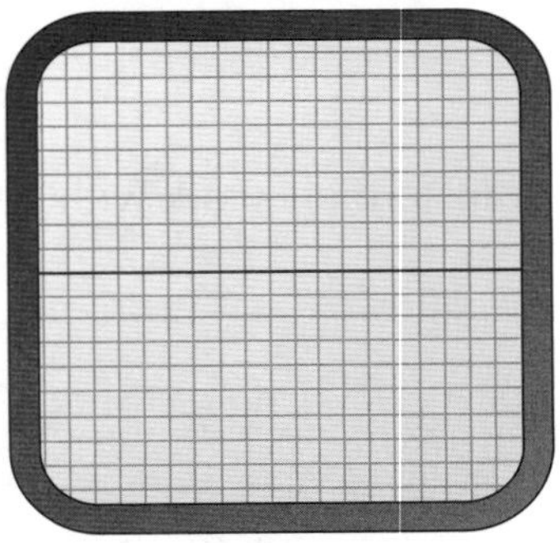

Transformers

Q1 Number the following statements in the **right order** from 1 to 5 to explain how a **transformer** works. The first one has been done for you.

	This causes a rapidly-changing magnetic field in the core.
	An alternating current can flow in a circuit connected to the secondary coil.
	An alternating current flows in the primary coil.
1	An alternating voltage is connected to the primary coil of a transformer.
	The changing magnetic field induces an alternating voltage in the secondary coil.

Q2 Tick the boxes to show whether these statements are **true** or **false**. Write out a **correct version** of each false statement.

True False

a) Transformers can work with AC or DC. ☐ ☐

....

b) A transformer consists of an iron core with one wire coil wound round it. ☐ ☐

....

c) Step-up transformers have less turns on the primary coil than the secondary coil. ☐ ☐

....

Q3 Transformers are made of a laminated **iron core** and **two coils** of wire.

a) Explain why a voltage is **induced** in the **secondary** coil when an **alternating** current flows in the **primary** coil.

....

....

....

....

b) Explain why transformers work with alternating current **only**.

....

....

....

Transformers

Q4 Ash, Lisa and Sara are discussing **transformers**.

Ash says: **"The core of a transformer has to be made of a conducting material such as iron so the current can get through."**

Lisa says: **"Transformers always have an equal number of turns on both coils."**

Sara says: **"Energy must pass through the core."**

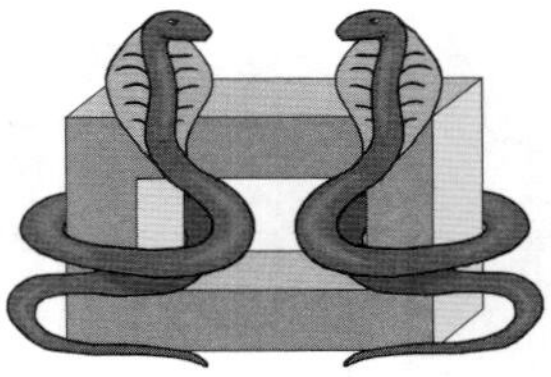

Who is **right** and who is **wrong**? Give **reasons** for your answers.

a) Ash is .... because ....

....

b) Lisa is .... because ....

....

c) Sara is .... because ....

....

Q5 Tim is investigating a transformer. He uses it to power a **spotlight**, and measures the **voltage** and **current** for both the primary and secondary coils. Here are his **results**:

Voltage to primary coil (V)	Current in primary coil (A)	Voltage to secondary coil (V)	Current in secondary coil (A)
240	0.25	12	5.0

a) Is Tim's transformer a **step-up** or **step-down** transformer? Give a reason for your answer.

....

b) **i)** Calculate the **power** in the **primary** coil when using the spotlight.

....

ii) Calculate the **power** the **secondary** coil when using the spotlight.

....

c) What idea about the **efficiency** of a transformer is confirmed by Tim's results?

....

Top Tips: Transformers — so much fun they had a whole cartoon series made about them. They had a nice equation made about them too — which awaits you on the next two pages. You'll also need to understand why transformers are used in the National Grid and in bathrooms. Handy.

More on Transformers

Q1 **Transformers** are very important for **power transmission** in the National Grid.

a) Fill in the **blanks** in the passage by choosing from the words below.

increase **generate** **decrease** **step-up** **step-down** **pipes** **cables**

.... transformers are used near power stations to ....
the voltage. The power is then carried through .... to near homes and
factories where .... transformers .... the voltage.

b) Indicate whether each statement is **true** or **false**. Write a **correct version** if the statement is false.

i) In transmission cables, higher voltage means lower current. **True / False**

....

ii) In transmission cables the energy lost is directly proportional to the current. **True / False**

....

Q2 Use the **transformer equation** to complete the following table.

Number of turns on primary coil	Voltage to primary coil (V)	Number of turns on secondary coil	Voltage to secondary coil (V)
1000	12	4000	
1000		2000	20
1000	12		12
	33 000	500	230

Q3 A transformer has **5000 turns** on its **primary** coil and **8000 turns** on its **secondary** coil.

a) If the **input** voltage is **230 V**, find the **output** voltage.

....

b) Andy builds a radio which needs a **20 V** electricity supply. The mains supply to a house is **230 V**. How could Andy adapt the transformer described above to make it suitable for his radio?

....

....

....

....

More on Transformers

Q4 **Isolating transformers** are safety devices.

a) Which sentence correctly states the **relationship** between the primary and secondary coils of an **isolating** transformer? Circle the correct letter.

A An isolating transformer has more turns on the primary coil than on the secondary coil.

B An isolating transformer has equal numbers of turns on the primary and secondary coils.

C An isolating transformer has more turns on the secondary coil than on the primary coil.

b) Do isolating transformers change the **voltage** in a circuit? ....

c) Explain why an isolating transformer is often used in a **bathroom** shaver circuit.

....

....

....

Q5 In one electricity distribution circuit, the cables carry a current of **200 A** at a voltage of **132 kV**.

a) Calculate the **power** transmitted by this circuit.

....

b) If a transformer is used to step the voltage down to **11 kV**, what will the **current** then be?

....

c) How is power **lost** during the transmission of electricity?

....

....

d) If the cables have a resistance of **0.3 Ω**, calculate how much power will be lost:

i) at a voltage of 132 kV.

....

ii) at a voltage of 11 kV.

....

e) Explain fully why the National Grid transmits electricity at **high voltage**.

....

....

....

Diodes and Rectification

Q1 Draw a line to match up each **keyword** with the correct **description**.

Keyword	Description
Semiconductor	has empty spaces called "holes" where electrons are missing
n-type semiconductor	conducts electricity but not as well as a conductor
p-type semiconductor	allows a current to flow in one direction only
Diode	has extra free electrons

Q2 a) Tick the boxes to show whether the following statements are **true** or **false**.

	True	False
i) The element silicon is a semiconductor.	☐	☐
ii) Semiconductors have low resistance in one direction and high resistance in the other.	☐	☐
iii) n-type semiconductors contain impurities but p-type semiconductors do not.	☐	☐
iv) 'Holes' effectively have a positive charge.	☐	☐
v) You need both p- and n-type semiconductors in a diode.	☐	☐

b) Write out **correct** versions of any false statements below.

....

....

....

....

....

Q3 Diodes can be used to **rectify** alternating current (AC).

a) i) What does '**rectification**' mean?

....

ii) Why is it sometimes necessary to rectify an alternating current (AC)?

....

b) Which method requires the **simplest** circuit — **half-wave** rectification or **full-wave** rectification?

....

c) How many diodes are required for full-wave rectification?

....

Diodes and Rectification

Q4 Describe what happens to the '**holes**' and electrons at the **p-n junction** in a diode when there is **no potential difference** across the diode.

Q5 Explain, in terms of the **movement of electrons**, why current flows in circuit **A** but not in circuit **B**.

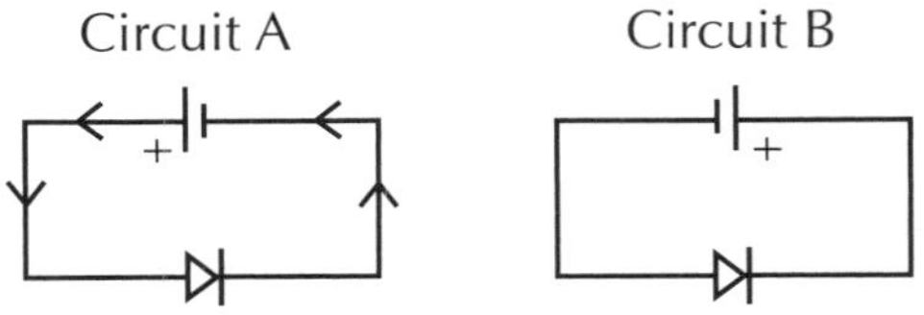

For this one, a sketched diagram on a bit of scrap paper might help. Or you could think about where the electrons "want" to go.

Q6 A single diode in series with an AC supply gives half-wave rectification.

a) Complete the diagram below to show the **output** voltage over **time** from the circuit shown.

HALF-WAVE RECTIFICATION

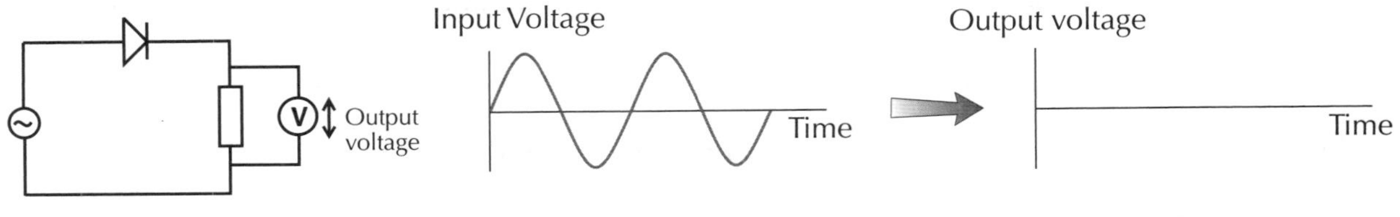

b) The diagram shows a **bridge** circuit which could be used to give **full-wave rectification**, but the **diodes** are missing.

Complete the diagram to show **the position of the diodes in circuit.**

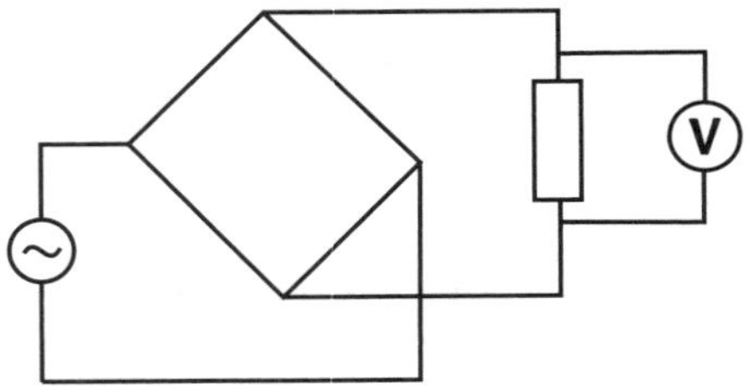

Top Tips: Yes, the circuit for Q6 b) is a bit of a pig. It's something that could come up in the exam, though, so be prepared to sketch it out and make sure you can explain how it works. It's well worth learning how p-type and n-type semiconductors make a diode work, they might pop up too.

Capacitors

Q1 a) Indicate whether the following statements are **true** or **false**.

	True	False
i) The higher the voltage of a power supply, the more charge a capacitor can store.	☐	☐
ii) A capacitor can be used to store electric current.	☐	☐

b) Write correct versions of any false statements below.

....

....

Q2 Over the last 50 years or so electronic **components** have become **smaller**, leading to smaller electronic devices being produced.

a) Give two possible **benefits** of smaller electronic devices.

1. ....

2. ....

b) Give two possible **drawbacks** of smaller electronic devices.

1. ....

2. ....

Q3 Capacitors are used in **smoothing circuits** like the one shown.

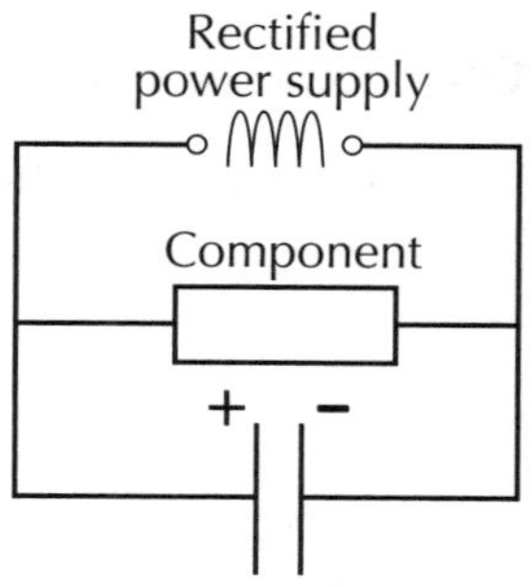

a) Explain why is it often **necessary** to **smooth** a rectified AC voltage?

....

....

b) Describe the current flow when the **input** voltage is **high**.

....

c) Describe the current flow when the **input** voltage is **low**.

....

d) Explain why the current through the component stays more or less **steady**.

....

....

....

Mixed Questions — Module P6

Q1 Emma did an experiment to test the **resistance** of two wires, **X** and **Y**.

a) Emma's results for wire **X** are shown on the **graph**. Use them to calculate the **resistance** of wire **X**.

....

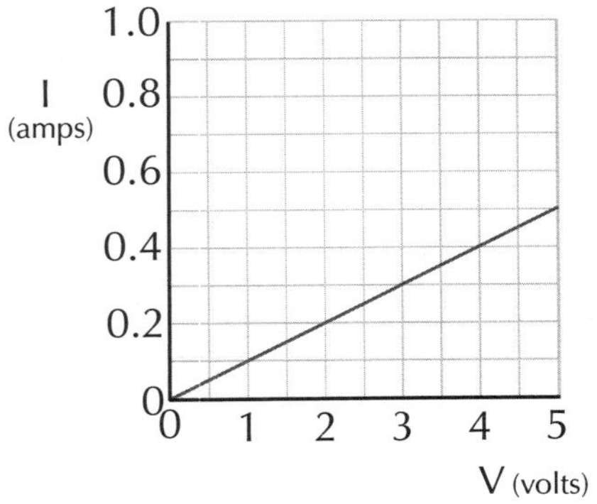

b) Wire **Y** has a resistance of **5 Ω**. Add the results you would **expect** for this wire to the **graph**.

c) Emma puts both wires in a circuit **together** as shown.

i) Calculate V_1 and V_2.

V_1 ....

V_2 ....

ii) What will be the value of V_{out}? ....

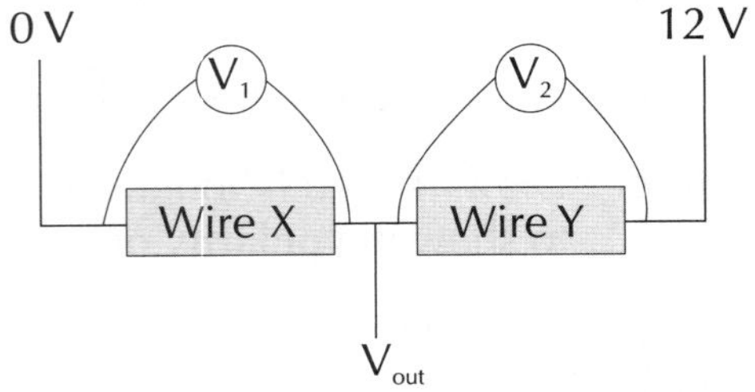

Q2 Bob wants a **warning light** to come on if a storeroom door is **closed** and the light inside is left **on**.

a) He realises that he needs to use **logic gates** in his system. Sadly he gets it **wrong** and sets up the system shown.

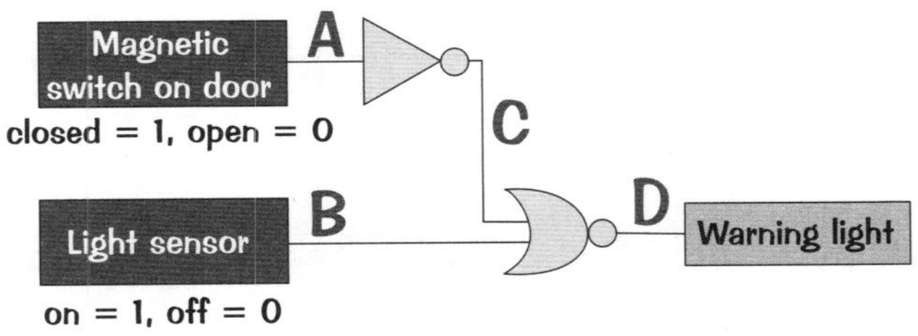

Inputs			Outputs
A	B	C	D

i) Fill in the **truth table** to show what happens in his system.

ii) In which **circumstances** will the light come **on**? ....

iii) Bob only actually needed to use **one logic gate**. Which was it? ....

b) Bob uses an **LDR** in the **potential divider** shown to **sense** whether the store room light is on. Explain how this works.

....

....

....

....

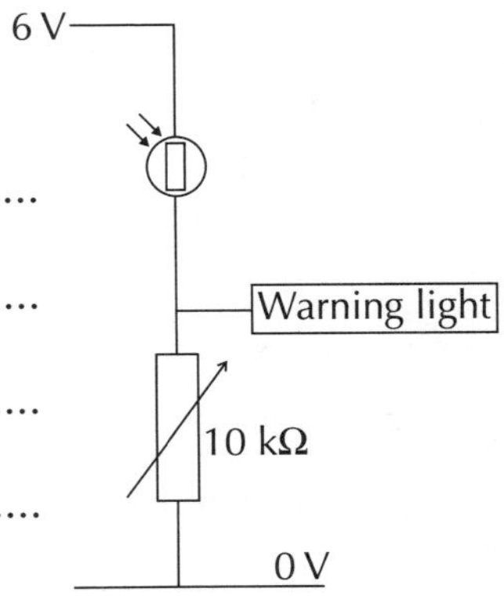

c) Bob decides he wants a **fan** to come on instead of the **warning light**. He discovers he needs to use a **relay**. Apart from safety considerations, why is this?

....

Mixed Questions — Module P6

Q3 The diagram below shows a simple **motor**. The coil is **rotating** as shown.

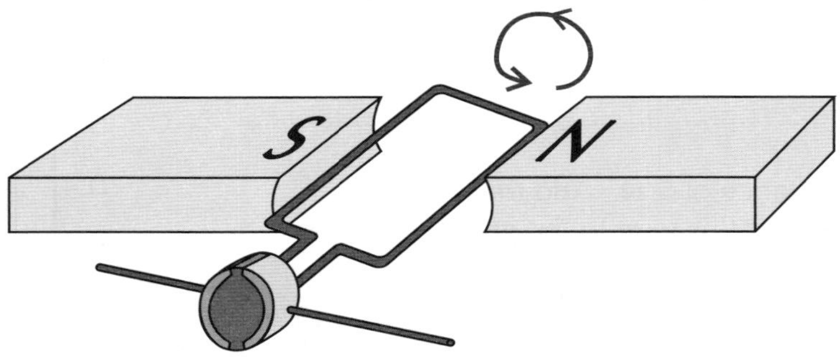

a) Draw arrows labelled '**F**' to show the direction of the force on **each arm** of the coil.

b) Draw arrows labelled '**I**' on each arm of the coil to show the direction the **current** is flowing.

c) Draw '**+**' and '**–**' on the leads of the **split-ring commutator** to show the **polarity** of the power supply.

d) Explain the advantage of using a **rectangular** coil in a motor.

....

e) The motor is connected to a **transformer**. Mains electricity supplies **230 V** to the **primary** coil which has **805 turns**. How many turns are on the **secondary** coil if the output voltage is **12 V**?

....

....

Q4 A radio requires a **direct current**. A **bridge circuit** is used to **rectify** the AC current supply.

a) Which **diodes** would the current flow through when:

i) X is **positive**? ....

ii) X is **negative**? ....

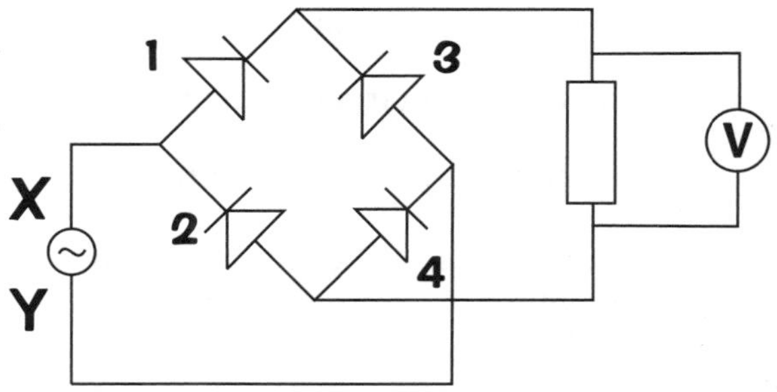

b) **Sketch** the **output** voltage you would expect from this circuit on the axes given

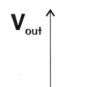

c) Before this electricity supply can be used for the radio it must be **smoothed**.

i) Add the smoothed voltage to the diagram in part **b)**.

ii) Name the **component** needed to smooth the voltage and draw its circuit **symbol**.

Component: .... Symbol: ....